Fors Clavigera. Letters to the Workmen and Labourers of Great Britain

John Ruskin

BIBLIOLIFE

FORS CLAVIGERA.

LETTERS

TO THE WORKMEN AND LABOURERS OF GREAT BRITAIN.

BY

JOHN RUSKIN, LL.D.,

HONORARY STUDENT OF CHRIST CHURCH, AND SLADE PROFESSOR OF FINE A

VOL. IV.

GEORGE ALLEN,
SUNNYSIDE, ORPINGTON, KENT.

1874

FORS CLAVIGERA.

FIRST SERIES.

CONTENTS OF VOL. IV. (1874.)

FORS CLAVIGERA.

LETTER THE 37th.

THE CITY WHICH IS OUR OWN

1st January, 1874

    " *Selon la loy, et ly prophetes,*
    Qui a charité parfaicte
    Il ayme Dieu sur toute rien
    De cueur, de force, et d'ame nette,
    Celui devons-nous tous de debte
    Comme soy-mesmes, son prochain,
    Qu'on dit qui m'ayme ayme mon chien.
    De tel pierre et de tel merrien
    Est ès cieulx nostre maison faicte
    Car nulz ne peut dire 'c'est mien,'
    Fors ce qu'il a mis en ce bien ;
    Tout le remenant est retraicte."

    According to the Law and the Prophets,
    He who has perfect charity,
    Loves God above everything
    With heart, with flesh, and with spirit pure
    Him also, our neighbour, we are all in debt
    To love as ourselves ,
    For one says, Who loves me loves my dog
    Of such stone, and of such crossbeam

Is in the heavens our house made;
For no one can say, ' It is mine,'
Beyond what he has put into that good;
All the rest is taken away.

ONE day last November, at Oxford, as I was going in
at the private door of the University galleries, to give a
lecture on the Fine Arts in Florence, I was hindered
for a moment by a nice little girl, whipping a top on the
pavement She was a *very* nice little girl ; and rejoiced
wholly in her whip, and top ; but could not inflict the
reviving chastisement with all the activity that was in
her, because she had on a large and dilapidated pair
of woman's shoes, which projected the full length of
her own little foot behind it and before , and being
securely fastened to her ankles in the manner of mo-
cassins, admitted, indeed, of dextrous glissades, and other
modes of progress quite sufficient for ordinary purposes ,
but not conveniently of all the evolutions proper to the
pursuit of a whipping-top.

There were some worthy people at my lecture, and I
think the lecture was one of my best. It gave some
really trustworthy information about art in Florence six
hundred years ago. But all the time I was speaking, I
knew that nothing spoken about art, either by myself
or other people, could be of the least use to anybody
there. For their primary business, and mine, was with
art in Oxford, now , not with art in Florence, then ;
and art in Oxford now was absolutely dependent on

our power of solving the question—which I knew that my audience would not even allow to be proposed for solution—"Why have our little girls large shoes ? "

Indeed, my great difficulty, of late, whether in lecturing or writing, is in the intensely practical and matter-of-fact character of my own mind as opposed to the loquacious and speculative disposition, not only of the British public, but of all my quondam friends. I am left utterly stranded, and alone, in life, and thought. Life and knowledge, I ought to say ; for I have done what thinking was needful for me long ago, and know enough to act upon, for the few days, or years, I may have yet to live. I find some of my friends greatly agitated in mind, for instance, about Responsibility, Free-will, and the like. I settled all those matters for myself, before I was ten years old, by jumping up and down an awkward turn of four steps in my nursery-stairs, and considering whether it was likely that God knew whether I should jump only three, or the whole four at a time. Having settled it in my mind that He knew quite well, though I didn't, which I should do , and also whether I should fall or not in the course of the performance,—though I was altogether responsible for taking care not to.—I never troubled my head more on the matter, from that day to this. But my friends keep buzzing and puzzling about it, as if they had to order the course of the world themselves ; and won't attend to me for an instant, if I ask why little girls have large shoes.

I don't suppose any man, with a tongue in his head, and zeal to use it, was ever left so entirely unattended to, as he grew old, by his early friends ; and it is doubly and trebly strange to me, because I have lost none of my power of sympathy with *them.* Some are chemists ; and I am always glad to hear of the last new thing in elements ; some are palæontologists, and I am no less happy to know of any lately unburied beast peculiar in his bones ; the lawyers and clergymen can always interest me with any story out of their courts or parishes ; —but not one of them ever asks what I am about myself. If they chance to meet me in the streets of Oxford, they ask whether I am staying there. When I say, yes, they ask how I like it ; and when I tell them I don't like it at all, and don't think little girls should have large shoes, they tell me I ought to read the 'Cours de Philosophie Positive.' As if a man who had lived to be fifty-four, content with what philosophy was needful to assure him that salt was savoury, and pepper hot, could ever be made positive in his old age, in the impertinent manner of these youngsters. But positive in a pertinent and practical manner, I have been, and shall be, with such stern and steady wedge of fact and act as time may let me drive into the gnarled blockheadism of the British mob.

I am free to confess I did not quite know the sort of creature I had to deal with, when I began, fifteen years ago, nor the quantity of ingenious resistance to practical reform which could be offered by theoretical reformers. Look, for instance, at this report of a speech of Mr. Bright's in the Times, on the subject of adulteration of food.*

" The noble lord has taken great pains upon this question, and has brought before the House a great amount of detail in connection with it. As I listened to his observations I hoped and believed that there was, though unintentional, no little exaggeration in them. Although there may be particular cases in which great harm to health and great fraud may possibly be shown, yet I think that general statements of this kind, implicating to a large extent the traders of this country, are dangerous, and are almost certain to be unjust. Now, my hon friend (Mr. Pochin) who has just addressed the House in a speech showing his entire mastery of the question, has confirmed my opinion, for he has shown—and I dare say he knows as much of the matter as any present—that there is a great deal of exaggeration in the opinions which have prevailed in many parts of the country, and which have even been found to prevail upon the matter in this House. . . . Now, I am prepared to show, that the exaggeration of the noble lord—I do not say intentionally, of course, I am sure he is incapable of that—is just as great in the matter of weights and measures as in that of adulteration. Probably he is not aware that in the list of persons employing weights that are inaccurate—I do not say fraudulent—no distinction is drawn between those who are intentionally fraudulent and those who are accidentally inaccurate, and that the penalty is precisely the same, and the offence is just as eagerly detected, whether there be a fraud or merely an accident Now, the noble lord will probably be surprised when I tell him that many persons

* Of 6th March, not long ago, but I have lost note of the year

are fined annually, not because their weights are too small, but because they are too large. In fact, when the weights are inaccurate, but are in favour of the customer, still the owner and user of the weight is liable to the penalty, and is fined. . . . My own impression with regard to this adulteration is that it arises from the very great, and perhaps inevitable, competition in business, and that to a great extent it is promoted by the ignorance of customers. As the ignorance of customers generally is diminishing, we may hope that before long the adulteration of food may also diminish. The noble lord appears to ask that something much more extensive and stringent should be done by Parliament. The fact is, it is vain to attempt by the power of Parliament to penetrate into and to track out evils such as those on which the noble lord has dwelt at such length. It is quite impossible that you should have the oversight of the shops of the country by inspectors, and that you should have persons going into shops to buy sugar, pickles, and Cayenne pepper, to get them analyzed, and then raise complaints against shopkeepers, and bring them before the magistrates. If men in their private businesses were to be tracked by Government officers and inspectors every hour of the day, life would not be worth having, and I recommend them to remove to another country, where they would not be subject to such annoyance."

Now, I neither know, nor does it matter to the public, what Mr. Bright actually said; but the report in the Times is the permanent and universally influential form of his sayings : and observe what the substance is, of these three or four hundred Parliamentary words, so reported.

First. That an evil which has been exaggerated ought not to be prevented.

Secondly. That at present we punish honest men as much as rogues; and must always continue to do so if we punish anybody.

Thirdly. That life would not be worth having if one's weights and measures were liable to inspection.

I can assure Mr. Bright that people who know what life means, can sustain the calamity of the inspection of their weights and measures with fortitude. I myself keep a tea-and-sugar shop. I have had my scales and weights inspected more than once or twice, and am not in the least disposed to bid my native land good-night on that account. That I could bid it nothing *but* good-night—never good-morning, the smoke of it quenching the sun, and its parliamentary talk, of such quality as the above, having become darkness voluble, and some of it worse even than that, a mere watchman's rattle, sprung by alarmed constituencies of rascals when an honest man comes in sight,—these are things indeed which should make any man's life little worth having, unless he separate himself from the scandalous crowd; but it must not be in exile from his country.

I have not hitherto stated, except in general terms, the design to which these letters point, though it has been again and again defined, and it seems to me explicitly enough—the highest possible education, namely, of English men and women living by agriculture in their native land. Indeed, during these three past years I have not hoped to do more than make my readers feel what mis-

chiefs they have to conquer   It is time now to say more
clearly what I want them to do.

The substantial wealth of man consists in the earth
he cultivates, with its pleasant or serviceable animals
and plants, and in the rightly produced work of his
own hands I mean to buy, for the St. George's
Company, the first pieces of ground offered to me at
fair price, (when the subscriptions enable me to give
any price,)—to put them as rapidly as possible into order,
and to settle upon them as many families as they can
support, of young and healthy persons, on the condition
that they do the best they can for their livelihood with
their own hands, and submit themselves and their children
to the rules written for them

I do not care where the land is, nor of what quality.
I would rather it should be poor, for I want space
more than food. I will make the best of it that I
can, at once, by wage-labour, under the best agricultural
advice It is easy now to obtain good counsel, and
many of our landlords would willingly undertake such
operations occasionally, but for the fixed notion that
every improvement of land should at once pay, whereas
the St George's Company is to be consistently monastic
in its principles of labour, and to work for the redemption
of any desert land, without other idea of gain than the
certainty of future good to others.   I should best like a
bit of marsh land of small value, which I would trench
into alternate ridge and canal, changing it all into solid

land, and deep water, to be farmed in fish If, instead, I get a rocky piece, I shall first arrange reservoirs for rain, then put what earth is sprinkled on it into workable masses ; and ascertaining, in either case, how many mouths the gained spaces of ground will easily feed, put upon them families chosen for me by old landlords, who know their people, and can send me cheerful and honest ones, accustomed to obey orders, and live in the fear of God Whether the fear be Catholic, or Church-of-England, or Presbyterian, I do not in the least care, so that the family be capable of any kind of sincere devotion ; and conscious of the sacredness of order. If any young couples of the higher classes choose to accept such rough life, I would rather have them for tenants than any others.

Tenants, I say, and at long lease, if they behave well. with power eventually to purchase the piece of land they live on for themselves, if they can save the price of it ; the rent they pay, meanwhile, being the tithe of the annual produce, to St. George's fund. The modes of the cultivation of the land are to be under the control of the overseer of the whole estate, appointed by the Trustees of the fund ; but the tenants shall build their own houses to their own minds, under certain conditions as to materials and strength ; and have for themselves the entire produce of the land, except the tithe aforesaid

The children will be required to attend training schools

for bodily exercise, and music, with such other education as I have already described. Every household will have its library, given it from the fund, and consisting of a fixed number of volumes,—some constant, the others chosen by each family out of a list of permitted books, from which they afterwards may increase their library if they choose. The formation of this library for choice, by a republication of classical authors in standard forms, has long been a main object with me. No newspapers, nor any books but those named in the annually renewed lists, are to be allowed in any household. In time I hope to get a journal published, containing notice of any really important matters taking place in this or other countries, in the closely sifted truth of them.

The first essential point in the education given to the children will be the habit of instant, finely accurate, and totally unreasoning, obedience to their fathers, mothers, and tutors; the same precise and unquestioning submission being required from heads of families to the officers set over them. The second essential will be the understanding of the nature of honour, making the obedience solemn and constant; so that the slightest wilful violation of the laws of the society may be regarded as a grave breach of trust, and no less disgraceful than a soldier's recoiling from his place in a battle.

In our present state of utter moral disorganization, it might indeed seem as if it would be impossible either to secure obedience, or explain the sensation of honour;

but the instincts of both are native in man, and the roots of them cannot wither, even under the dust-heap of modern liberal opinions. My settlers, you observe, are to be young people, bred on old estates ; my commandants will be veteran soldiers ; and it will be soon perceived that pride based on servitude to the will of another is far loftier and happier than pride based on servitude to humour of one's own.

Each family will at first be put on its trial for a year, without any lease of the land : if they behave well, they shall have a lease for three years ; if through that time they satisfy their officers, a life-long lease, with power to purchase.

I have already stated that no machines moved by artificial power are to be used on the estates of the society ; wind, water, and animal force are to be the only motive powers employed, and there is to be as little trade or importation as possible ; the utmost simplicity of life, and restriction of possession, being combined with the highest attainable refinement of temper and thought. Everything that the members of any household can sufficiently make for themselves, they are so to make, however clumsily ; but the carpenter and smith, trained to perfectest work in wood and iron, are to be employed on the parts of houses and implements in which finish is essential to strength. The ploughshare and spade must be made by the smith, and the roof and floors by a carpenter ; but the boys of the house must be able to make either a horseshoe, or a table.

Simplicity of life without coarseness, and delight in life without lasciviousness, are, under such conditions, not only possible to human creatures, but natural to them. I do not pretend to tell you straightforwardly all laws of nature respecting the conduct of men; but some of those laws I know, and will endeavour to get obeyed; others, as they are needful, will be in the sequel of such obedience ascertained. What final relations may take place between masters and servants, labourers and employers, old people and young, useful people and useless, in such a society, only experience can conclude; nor is there any reason to anticipate the conclusion. Some few things the most obstinate will admit, and the least credulous believe: that washed faces are healthier than dirty ones, whole clothes decenter than ragged ones, kind behaviour more serviceable than malicious, and pure air pleasanter than foul. Upon that much of 'philosophie positive' I mean to act; and, little by little, to define in these letters the processes of action. That it should be left to me to begin such a work, with only one man in England—Thomas Carlyle—to whom I can look for steady guidance, is alike wonderful and sorrowful to me; but as the thing is so, I can only do what seems to me necessary, none else coming forward to do it. For my own part, I entirely hate the whole business: I dislike having either power or responsibility; am ashamed to ask for money, and plagued in spending it. I don't want to talk, nor to write, nor to advise or direct anybody. I am far more provoked at being thought foolish by foolish people, than pleased at being thought sensible by sensible people ; and the average proportion of the numbers of each is not to my advantage. If I could find anyone able to carry on the plan instead of me, I never should trouble myself about it more ; and even now, it is only with extreme effort and chastisement of my indolence that I go on : but, unless I am struck with palsy, I do not seriously doubt my perseverance, until I find somebody able to take up the matter in the same mind, and with a better heart.

The laws required to be obeyed by the families living on the land will be,—with some relaxation and modification, so as to fit them for English people,—those of Florence in the fourteenth century. In what additional rules may be adopted, I shall follow, for the most part, Bacon, or Sir Thomas More, under sanction always of the higher authority which of late the English nation has wholly set its strength to defy—that of the Founder of its Religion ; nor without due acceptance of what teaching was given to the children of God by their Father, before the day of Christ, of which, for present ending, read and attend to these following quiet words.*

* The close of the ninth book of Plato's Republic I use for the most part Mr Jowett's translation, here and there modifying it in my own arbitrarily dogged or diffuse way of Englishing passages of complex significance.

"' In what point of view, then, and on what ground shall a man be profited by injustice or intemperance or other baseness, even though he acquire money or power ? '

' There is no ground on which this can be maintained.'

' What shall he profit if his injustice be undetected ? for he who is undetected only gets worse, whereas he who is detected and punished has the brutal part of his nature silenced and humanized ; the greater element in him is liberated, and his whole soul is perfected and ennobled by the acquirement of justice and temperance and wisdom, more than the body ever is by receiving gifts of beauty, strength, and health, in proportion as the soul is more honourable than the body.'

' Certainly,' he said.

' Will not, then, the man of understanding, gather all that is in him, and stretch himself like a bent bow to this aim of life ; and, in the first place, honour studies which thus chastise and deliver his soul in perfection ; and despise others?'

' Clearly,' he said.

' In the next place, he will keep under his body, and so far will he be from yielding to brutal and irrational pleasure,* that he will not even first look to bodily health as his main object, nor desire to be fair, or strong, or well, unless he is likely thereby to gain tem-

---

* Plato does not mean here, merely dissipation of a destructive kind, (as the next sentence shows,) but also healthy animal stupidities, as our hunting, shooting. and the like.

perance ; but he will be always desirous of preserving the harmony of the body for the sake of the concord of the soul ?'

' Certainly,' he replied, ' that he will, if he is indeed taught by the Muses.'

' And he will also observe the principle of classing and concord in the acquisition of wealth ; and will not, because the mob beatify him, increase his endless load of wealth to his own infinite harm ?'

' I think not,' he said.

' He will look at the city which is within him, and take care to avoid any change of his own institutions, such as might arise either from abundance or from want ; and he will duly regulate his acquisition and expense, in so far as he is able ?'

' Very true.'

' And, for the same reason, he will accept such honours as he deems likely to make him a better man ; but those which are likely to loosen his possessed habit, whether private or public honours, he will avoid ?'

' Then, if this be his chief care, he will not be a politician ?'

' By the dog of Egypt, he will ! in the city which is his own, though in his native country perhaps not, unless some providential accident should occur.'

' I understand ; you speak of that city of which we are the founders, and which exists in idea only, for I do not think there is such an one anywhere on earth ?'

'In heaven,' I replied, 'there is laid up a pattern of such a city; and he who desires may behold this, and, beholding, govern himself accordingly. But whether there really is, or ever will be, such an one, is of no importance to him, for he will act accordingly to the laws of that city and of no other?'

'True,' he said."

NOTES AND CORRESPONDENCE.

It is due to my readers to state my reasons for raising the price, and withdrawing the frontispieces, of Fors.

The cessation of the latter has nothing to do with the price. At least, for the raised price I could easily afford the plates, and they would help the sale; but I cannot spare my good assistant's time in their preparation, and find that, in the existing state of trade, I cannot trust other people, without perpetual looking after them; for which I have no time myself. Even last year the printing of my Fors frontispieces prevented the publication of my Oxford lectures on engraving; and it is absolutely necessary that my Oxford work should be done rightly, whatever else I leave undone. Secondly, for the rise in price. I hold it my duty to give my advice for nothing, but not to write it in careful English, and correct press, for nothing. I like the feeling of being paid for my true work as much as any other labourer; and though I write Fors, not for money, but because I know it to be wanted, as I would build a wall against the advancing sea for nothing, if I couldn't be paid for doing it; yet I will have proper pay from the harbour-master, if I can get it. As soon as the book gives me and the publisher what is right, the surplus shall go to the St George's fund. The price will not signify ultimately,—sevenpence, or tenpence, or a shilling, will be all the same to the public if the book is found useful,—but I fix, and mean to keep to, tenpence, because I intend striking for use on my farms the pure silver coin called in Florence the 'soldo,' of which the golden florin was worth twenty, (the soldo itself being misnamed from the Roman 'solidus') and this soldo will represent the Roman denarius, and be worth ten silver pence, and this is to be the price of Fors.

Then one further *petty* reason I have for raising the price. In all my dealings with the public, I wish them to understand that my first price is my lowest. They may have to pay more; but never a farthing less And I am a little provoked at not having been helped in the least by the Working Men's College, after I taught there for five years, or by any of my old pupils there, whom I have lost sight of·—(three remain who would always help me in anything,) and I think they will soon begin to want Fors, now,—and they shall not have it for seven-pence.

The following three stray newspaper cuttings may as well be printed now; they have lain some time by me The first two relate to economy. The last is, I hope, an exaggerated report, and I give it as an example of the kind of news which my own journal will *not* give on hearsay. But I know that things did take place in India which were not capable of exaggeration in horror, and such are the results, remember, of our past missionary work, as a whole, in India and China.

I point to them to-day, in order that I may express my entire concurrence in all that I have seen reported of Professor Max Müller's lecture in Westminster Abbey, though there are one or two things I should like to say in addition, if I can find time

" Those who find fault with the present Government on account of its rigid economy, and accuse it of shabbiness, have little idea of the straits it is put to for money and the sacrifices it is obliged to make in order to make both ends meet The following melancholy facts will serve to show how hardly pushed this great nation is to find sixpence even for a good purpose. The Hakluyt Society was, as some of our readers may know, formed in the year 1846 for the purpose of printing in English for distribution among its members rare and valuable voyages, travels, and geographical records, including the more important early narratives of British enterprise. For many years the Home Office, the Board of Trade, and the Admiralty have been in the habit of subscribing for the publications of this society; and considering that an annual subscription of one guinea entitles each subscriber to receive without further charge a copy of every work produced by the society within the year subscribed for, it can hardly be said that the outlay was ruinous to the Exchequer. But we live in an exceptional period: and accordingly last year the society received a communication from the Board of Trade to the effect that its publications were no longer required. Then the Home Office wrote to say that its subscription must be discontinued, and followed up the communication by another, asking whether it might have a copy of the society's publications, supplied to it gratuitously. Lastly, the Admiralty felt itself constrained by the urgency of the times to reduce its subscription, and asked to have only one instead of two copies annually. It seems rather hard on the Hakluyt Society that the Home Office should beg to have its publications for nothing, and for the sake of appearance it seems advisable that the Admiralty should continue its subscription for two copies, and lend one set to its impoverished brother in Whitehall until the advent of better times." — *Pall Mall Gazette.*

" We make a present of a suggestion to Professor Beesly, Mr. Frederic Harrison, and the artisans who are calling upon the country to strike a blow for France. They must appoint a Select Committee to see what war really means. Special commissioners will find out for them how many pounds, on an average, have been lost by the families whose breadwinners have gone to Paris with the King, or to Le Mans with Chanzy. Those hunters of facts will also let the working men know how many fields are unsown round Metz and on the Loire. Next, the Select Committee will get an exact return of the killed and wounded from Count Bismarck and M. Gambetta. Some novelist or poet—a George Eliot or a Browning—will then be asked to lavish all the knowledge of human emotion in the painting of one family group out of the half-million which the returns of the stricken will show. That picture will be distributed broadcast among the working men and their wives. Then the Select Committee will call to its aid the statisticians and the political economists—the Leone Levis, and the John Stuart Mills. Those authorities will calculate what sum the war has taken from the wages fund of France and Germany; what number of working men it will cast out of employment, or force to accept lower wages, or compel to emigrate." (I do not often indulge myself in the study of the works of Mr. Levi or Mr Mill ;—but have they really never done anything of this kind hitherto ?) "Thus the facts will be brought before the toiling people, solidly, simply, truthfully. Finally, Professor Beesly and Mr. Harrison will call another meeting, will state the results of the investigation, will say, ' This is the meaning of war,' and will ask the workmen whether they are prepared to pay the inevitable price of helping Republican France. The answer, we imagine, would at once shock and surprise the scholarly gentlemen to whom the Democrats are indebted for their logic and their rhetoric. Meanwhile Mr Ruskin and the Council of the Workmen's National Peace Society have been doing some small measure of the task which we have mapped out. The Council asks the bellicose section of the operative classes a number of questions about the cost and the effect of battles. Some, it is true, are not very cogent, and some are absurd, but, taken together, they press the inquiry whether war

pays anybody, and in particular whether it pays the working man.
Mr. Ruskin sets forth the truth much more vividly in the letter
which appeared in our impression of Thursday. 'Half the money
lost by the inundation of the Tiber,' etc., (the Telegraph quotes
the letter to the end)

" Before stating what might have been done with the force which
has been spent in the work of mutual slaughter, Mr. Ruskin might
have explained what good it has undone, and how. Take, first,
the destruction of capital. Millions of pounds have been spent
on gunpowder, bombs, round shot, cannon, needle guns, chassepôts, and mitrailleuses. But for the war, a great part of the sum
would have been expended in the growing of wheat, the spinning
of cloth, the building of railway bridges, and the construction of
ships. As the political economists say, the amount would have
been spent productively, or, to use the plain words of common
speech, would have been so used that, directly or indirectly, it
would have added to the wealth of the country, and increased
the fund to be distributed among the working people. But the
wealth has been blown away from the muzzle of the cannon, or
scattered among the woods and forts of Paris in the shape of
broken shells and dismounted guns. Now, every shot which is
fired is a direct loss to the labouring classes of France and
Germany. *King William on the one side, and General Trochu on
the other, really load their guns with gold.* They put the wages of
the working people into every shell. The splinters of iron that
strew the fields represent the pay which would have gone to the
farm labourers of Alsace, the mechanics of Paris and Berlin, and
the silk weavers of Lyons. If the political economist were some
magician, he would command the supernatural agent to transform
the broken gun-carriages, the fragments of bombs, and the round
shot into loaves of bread, bottles of wine, fields of corn, clothes,
houses, cattle, furniture, books, the virtue of women, the health
of children, the years of the aged. The whole field would become

alive with the forms, the wealth, the beauty, the bustle of great cities. If working men ever saw such a transformation, they would rise up from end to end of Europe, and execrate the King or Emperor who should let loose the dogs of war. And yet such a scene would represent only a small part of the real havoc. For every man whom Germany takes away from the field or the workshop to place in the barrack or the camp, she must sustain as certain a loss as if she were to cast money into the sea. The loss may be necessary as an insurance against still greater injury, but nevertheless the waste does take place, and on the working people does it mainly fall. The young recruit may have been earning thirty shillings a week or a day, and that sum is lost to himself or his friends. Hitherto he has supported himself; now he must be maintained by the State—that is, by his fellow-subjects. Hitherto he has added to the national wealth by ploughing the fields, building houses, constructing railways. A skilful statistician could state, with some approach to accuracy, the number of pounds by which the amount of his yearly productive contribution could be estimated It might be thirty, or a hundred, or a thousand. Well, he ceases to produce the moment that he becomes a soldier. He is then a drone. He is as unproductive as a pauper. The millions of pounds spent in feeding and drilling the army as clearly represent a dead loss as the millions spent on workhouses. Nor are these the only ways in which war destroys wealth. Hundreds of railway bridges have been broken down; the communications between different parts of the country have been cut off, hundreds of thousands have lost their means of livelihood, and great tracts of country are wasted like a desert. Thus the total destruction of wealth has been appalling. A considerable time ago Professor Leone Levi calculated that Germany alone had lost more than £300,000,000, France must have lost much more; and, even if we make a liberal discount from so tremendous a computation, we may safely say that the war has cost both nations at least half as much as the National Debt of England.

"A large part of that amount, it is true, would have been spent unproductively, even if the war had not taken place. A vast sum would have been lavished on the luxuries of dress and the table, on the beauties of art, and on the appliances of war. But it is safe to calculate that at least half of the amount would have been so expended as to bring a productive return. Two or three hundred millions would have been at the service of peace, and Mr. Ruskin's letter points the question, What could have been done with that enormous total? If it were at the disposal of an English statesman as far-seeing in peace as Bismarck is in war, what might not be done for the England of the present and the future? The prospect is almost millennial. Harbours of refuge might be built all round the coast; the fever dens of London, Manchester, and Liverpool might give place to abodes of health; the poor children of the United Kingdom might be taught to read and write; great universities might be endowed, the waste lands might be cultivated, and the Bog of Allen drained; the National Debt could be swiftly reduced; and a hundred other great national enterprises would sooner or later be fulfilled. But all this store of human good has been blown away from the muzzles of the Krupps and the chassepôts. It has literally been transformed into smoke. We do not deny that such a waste may be necessary in order to guard against still further destruction. Wars have often been imperative. It would frequently be the height of national wickedness to choose an ignoble peace. Nevertheless war is the most costly and most wasteful of human pursuits When the working class followers of Professor Beesly ask themselves what is the price of battle, what it represents, and by whom the chief part is paid, they will be better able to respond to the appeal for armed intervention than they were on Tuesday night."
—*Daily Telegraph, January* 14*th*, 1871.

"The story of the massacre of Tientsin, on the 21st June last, is told in a private letter dated Cheefoo, June 30th, published in Thursday's Standard, but the signature of which is not given. The horrors narrated are frightful, and remembering how frequently stories of similar horrors in the Mutiny melted away on close investigation,—though but too many were true,—we may hope that the writer, who does not seem to have been in Tientsin at the time, has heard somewhat exaggerated accounts. Yet making all allowances for this, there was evidently horror enough. The first attack was on the French Consul, who was murdered, the Chinese mandarins refusing aid. Then the Consulate was broken open, and two Catholic priests murdered, as well as M. and Madame Thomassin, an attaché to the Legation at Pekin and his bride. Then came the worst part. The mob, acting with regular Chinese soldiers, it is said, whom their officers did not attempt to restrain, attacked the hospital of the French Sisters of Charity, stripped them, exposed them to the mob, plucked out their eyes, multilated them in other ways, and divided portions of their flesh among the infuriated people, and then set fire to the hospital, in which a hundred orphan children, who were the objects of the sisters' care, were burnt to death."—*The Spectator, September 3rd, 1870.*

FORS CLAVIGERA.

LETTER THE 38th.

"CHILDREN, HAVE YOU HERE ANY MEAT?"

HERNE HILL, *December*, 1873.

THE laws of Florence in the fourteenth century, for us in the nineteenth!

Even so, good reader. You have, perhaps, long imagined that the judges of Israel, and heroes of Greece, the consuls of Rome, and the dukes of Venice, the powers of Florence, and the kings of England, were all merely the dim foreshadowings and obscure prophecyings of the advent of the Jones and Robinson of the future. demi-gods revealed in your own day, whose demi-divine votes, if luckily coincident upon any subject, become totally divine, and establish the ordinances thereof, for ever.

You will find it entirely otherwise, gentlemen, whether of the suburb, or centre. Laws small and great, for ever unchangeable,—irresistible by all the force of Robinson, and unimprovable by finest jurisprudence of Jones, have long since been known, and, by wise nations, obeyed.

Out of the statute books of one of these I begin with an apparently unimportant order, but the sway of it cuts deep.

"No person whatsoever shall buy fish, to sell it again, either in the market of Florence, or in any markets in the state of Florence."

It is one of many such laws, entirely abolishing the profession of middleman, or costermonger of perishable articles of food, in the city of the Lily.

"Entirely abolishing,—nonsense!" thinks your modern commercial worship. "Who was to prevent private contract?"

Nobody, my good sir;—there is, as you very justly feel, no power in law whatever to prevent private contract. No quantity of laws, penalties, or constitutions, can be of the slightest use to a public inherently licentious and deceitful. There is no legislation for liars and traitors. They cannot be prevented from the pit; the earth finally swallows them. They find their level against all embankment—soak their way down, irrestrainably, to the gutter grating,—happiest the nation that most rapidly so gets rid of their stench. There is no law, I repeat, for these, but gravitation. Organic laws can only be serviceable to, and in general will only be written by, a public of honourable citizens, loyal to their state, and faithful to each other.

The profession of middleman was then, by civic consent, and formal law, rendered impossible in Florence with respect to fish. What advantage the modern blessed possibility of such mediatorial function brings to our hungry multitudes ; and how the miraculous draught of fishes, which living St. Peter discerns, and often dextrously catches—" the shoals of them like shining continents," (said Carlyle to me, only yesterday,)—are by such apostolic succession miraculously diminished, instead of multiplied ; and, instead of baskets full of fragments taken up from the ground, baskets full of whole fish laid down on it, lest perchance any hungry person should cheaply eat of the same,—here is a pleasant little account for you, by my good and simple clergyman's wife. It would have been better still, if I had not been forced to warn her that I wanted it for Fors, which of course took the sparkle out of her directly. Here is one little naughty bit of private preface, which really must go with the rest. " I have written my little letter about the fish trade, and L. says it is all right. I am afraid you won't think there is anything in it worth putting in Fors, as I really know very little about it, and absolutely nothing that every one else does not know, except ladies, who generally never trouble about anything, but scold their cooks, and abuse the fishmongers—when they cannot pay the weekly bills easily." (After this we are quite proper.)

" The poor fishermen who toil all through these bitter nights, and the retail dealer who carries heavy baskets, or drags a truck so many weary miles along the roads, get but a poor living out of their labour ; but what are called ‘fish salesmen,’ who by reason of their command of capital keep entire command of the London markets, are making enormous fortunes.

"When you ask the fishermen why they do not manage better for themselves at the present demand for fish, they explain how helpless they are in the hands of what they call ‘the big men.’ Some fishermen at Aldborough, who have a boat of their own, told my brother that one season, when the sea seemed full of herrings, they saw in the newspapers how dear they were in London, and resolved to make a venture on their own account ; so they spent all their available money in the purchase of a quantity of the right sort of baskets, and, going out to sea, filled them all,—putting the usual five hundred lovely fresh fish in each,—sent them straight up to London by train, to the charge of a salesman they knew of, begging him to send them into the market and do the best he could for them But he was very angry with the fishermen ; and wrote them word that the market was quite sufficiently stocked ; that if more fish were sent in, *the prices would go down ;* that he should not allow their fish to be sold at all ; and, if they made a fuss about it, he would not send their baskets back, and would make them pay the carriage. As it was, he returned them, after a time ; but the poor men never received one farthing for their thousands of nice fish, and only got a scolding for having dared to try and do without the agents who buy the fish from the boats at whatever price they choose to settle amongst themselves

"When we were at Yarmouth this autumn, the enormous abundance of herrings on the fish quay was perfectly wonderful ; it must be, (I should think,) two hundred yards long, and is capable of accommodating the unloading of a perfect fleet of boats. The 'swills,' as they call the baskets, each containing five hundred fish, were side by side, touching each other, all over this immense space, and men were shovelling salt about, with spades, over heaps of fish, previous to packing at once in boxes. I said, ' How surprised our poor people would be to see such a sight, after constantly being obliged to pay three-halfpence for every herring they buy.' An old fisherman answered me, saying, 'No one need pay that, ma'am, if we could get the fish to them ; we could have plenty more boats, and plenty more fish, if we could have them taken where the poor people could get them' We brought home a hundred dried herrings, for which we paid ten shillings ; when we asked if we might buy some lovely mackerel on the Fish Quay, they said, (the fishermen,) that they were not allowed to sell them there, except all at once. Since then, I have read an account of a Royal Commission having been investigating the subject of the fishery for some time past, and the result of its inquiries seems to prove that it is inexhaustible, and that in the North Sea it is always harvest-time.*

"When I told our fishmonger all about it, he said I was quite right about the 'big men' in London, and added, 'They will not let us have the fish under their own prices; and if it is so plentiful that they cannot sell it all at that, they have it thrown away, or carted off for manure, sometimes sunk in the river. If we could only get it here, my trade would be twice what it is, for, except sprats, the poor can seldom buy fish now.'

---

* Not quite so, gentlemen of the Royal Commission. Harvests, no less than sales, and fishermen no less than salesmen, need regulation by just human law. Here is a piece of news, for instance, from Glasgow, concerning Loch Fyne.—"Owing to the permission to fish for herring by trawling, which not only scrapes up the spawn from the bottom, but catches great quantities of the fry, which are useless for market, and only fit for manure, it is a fact that, whereas Loch Fyne used to be celebrated for containing the finest herrings to be caught anywhere, and thousands and tens of thousands of boxes used to be exported from Inverary, there are not now enough caught there to *enable them to export a single box*, and the quantity caught lower down the loch, near its mouth (and every year the herring are being driven farther and farther down) is not a tithe of what it used to be. Such a thing as a Loch Fyne herring (of the old size and quality) cannot be had now in Glasgow for any money, and this is only a type of the destruction which trawling, and too short close-time, are causing to all the west-coast fishing. Whiting Bay, Arran, has been rid of its whiting by trawling on the spawning coast opposite. The cupidity of careless fishers, unchecked by beneficial law, is here also 'killing the goose that lays the golden eggs,' and herring of any kind are *very* scarce and very bad in Glasgow, at a penny and sometimes twopence each. Professor Huxley gave his sanction to trawling, in a Government Commission, I am told, some years ago, and it has been allowed ever since. I will tell you something similar about the seal-fishing off Newfoundland, another time."

"I asked him if the new Columbia Market was of no use in making things easier, but he said, 'No;' that these salesmen had got that into their hands also; and were so rich that they would keep any number of markets in their own hands. A few hundred pounds sacrificed any day to keep up the prices they think well worth their while."

What do you think of that, by way of Free-trade?—my British-never-never-never-will-be-slaves,—hey? Free-trade; and the Divine Law of Supply and Demand; and the Sacred Necessity of Competition, and what not;—and here's a meek little English housewife who can't get leave, on her bended knees, from Sultan Costermonger, to eat a fresh herring at Yarmouth! and must pay three-half-pence apiece, for his leave to eat them anywhere;—and you, you simpletons—Fishermen, indeed!—Cod's heads and shoulders, say rather,—meekly receiving back your empty baskets; your miracle of loaves and fishes executed for you by the Costermongering Father of the Faithful, in that thimblerig manner!

"But haven't you yourself been hard against competition, till now? and haven't *you* always wanted to regulate prices?"

Yes, my good SS. Peter and Andrew!—very certainly I want to regulate prices; and very certainly I will, as to such things as I sell, or have the selling of. I should like to hear of anybody's getting this letter for less than tenpence !—and if you will send *me* some fish to sell for you, perhaps I may even resolve that they shall be sold at twopence each, or else made manure of,— like these very costermongers ; but the twopence shall go into your pockets—not mine ; which you will find a very pleasant and complete difference in principle between his Grace the Costermonger and me , and, secondly, if I raise the price of a herring to twopence, it will be because I know that people have been in some way misusing them, or wasting them , and need to get fewer for a time , or will eat twopenny herrings at fashionable tables, (when they wouldn't touch half-penny ones,) and so give the servants no reason to turn up their noses at them.* I may have twenty such good reasons for fixing the price of your fish ; but not one of them will be his Grace the Costermonger's All that I want you to see is, not only the possibility of regulating prices, but the fact that they *are* now regulated, and regulated by rascals, while all the world is bleating out its folly about Supply and Demand.

"Still, even in your way, you would be breaking the laws of Florence, anyhow, and buying to sell again ?" Pardon me . I should no more buy your fish than a butcher's boy buys his master's mutton I should simply carry your fish for you where I knew it was wanted ;

---

* In my aunt's younger days, at Perth, the servants used regularly to make bargain that they should not be forced to dine on salmon more than so many times a week.

being as utterly your servant in the matter as if I were one of your own lads sent dripping up to the town with basket on back. And I should be paid, as your servant, so much wages ; (not *commission*, observe,) making bargains far away for you, and many another Saunders Mucklebackit, just as your wife makes them, up the hill at Monkbarns ; and no more buying the fish, to sell again, than she.

" Well, but where could we get anybody to do this ? "

Have you no sons then ?—or, among them, none whom you can take from the mercy of the sea, and teach to serve you mercifully on the land ?

It is not that way, however, that the thing will be done. It must be done for you by gentlemen. They may stagger on perhaps a year or two more in their vain ways ; but the day *must* come when your poor little honest puppy, whom his people have been wanting to dress up in a surplice, and call, " The to be Feared," that he might have pay enough, by tithe or tax, to marry a pretty girl, and live in a ,parsonage,—some poor little honest wretch of a puppy, I say, will eventually get it into his glossy head that he would be incomparably more reverend to mortals, and acceptable to St. Peter and all Saints, as a true monger of sweet fish, than a false fisher for rotten souls ; and that his wife would be incomparably more ' lady-like '—not to say Madonna-like—marching beside him in purple stockings and sabots—or even frankly barefoot—with her creel full of caller herring on her back, than in administering any quantity of Ecclesiastical scholarship to her Sunday-schools.

" How dreadful—how atrocious ! "—thinks the tender clerical lover. " *My* wife walk with a fish-basket on her back ! "

Yes, you young scamp, yours. You were going to lie to the Holy Ghost, then, were you, only that she might wear satin slippers and be called a ' lady ' ? Suppose, instead of fish, I were to ask her and you to carry coals. Have you ever read your Bible carefully enough to wonder where Christ got them from, to make His fire, (when He was so particular about St. Peter's dinner, and St. John's) ? Or if I asked you to be hewers of wood, and drawers of water ,—would that also seem intolerable to you ? My poor clerical friends, God was never more in the burning bush of Sinai than He would be in every crackling faggot (cut with your own hands) that you warmed a poor hearth with : nor did that woman of Samaria ever give Him to drink more surely than you may, from every stream and well in this your land, that you can keep pure.

20*th Dec*—To hew wood—to draw water ,—you think these base businesses, do you ? and that you are noble, as well as sanctified, in binding faggot-burdens on poor men's backs, which you will not touch with your own fingers ,—and in preaching the efficacy of baptism inside the church, by yonder stream (under the first bridge of the Seven Bridge Road here at Oxford,) while the sweet waters of it are choked with dust and dung, within ten fathoms from your font;—and in giving benediction with two fingers and your thumb, of a superfine quality, to the Marquis of B. ? Honester benediction, and more efficacious, can be had cheaper, gentlemen, in the existing market. Under my own system of regulating prices, I gave an Irishwoman twopence yesterday for two oranges, of which fruit—under pressure of competition—she was ready to supply me with three for a penny. " The Lord Almighty take you to eternal glory ! " said she.

You lawyers, also,—distributors, by your own account, of the quite supreme blessing of Justice,—you are not so busily eloquent in her cause but that some of your sweet voices might be spared to Billingsgate, though the river air might take the curl out of your wigs, and so diminish that æsthetic claim, which, as aforesaid, you still hold on existence. But you will bring yourselves to an end soon,—wigs and all,—unless you think better of it.

I will dismiss at once, in this letter, the question of regulation of prices, and return to it no more, except in setting down detailed law

Any rational group of persons, large or small, living in war or peace, will have its commissariat ,—its officers for provision of food. Famine in a fleet, or an army, may sometimes be inevitable ; but in the event of *national* famine, the officers of the commissariat should be starved the first. God has given to man corn, wine, cheese, and

honey, all preservable for a number of years;—filled
His seas with inexhaustible salt, and incalculable fish;
filled the woods with beasts, the winds with birds, and
the fields with fruit. Under these circumstances, the
stupid human brute stands talking metaphysics, and
expects to be fed by the law of Supply and Demand.
I do not say that I shall always succeed in regulating
prices, or quantities, absolutely to my mind; but in the
event of any scarcity of provision, rich tables shall be
served like the poorest, and—we will see.

The price of every other article will be founded on
the price of food. The price of what it takes a day to
produce, will be a day's maintenance; of what it takes
a week to produce, a week's maintenance,—such maintenance being calculated according to the requirements of
the occupation, and always with a proportional surplus
for saving.

"How am I to know exactly what a day's maintenance is?" I don't want to know exactly. I don't know
exactly how much dinner I ought to eat; but, on the
whole, I eat enough, and not too much. And I shall
not know 'exactly' how much a painter ought to have
for a picture. It may be a pound or two under the mark
—a pound or two over. On the average it will be right,
—that is to say, his decent keep * during the number of

* As for instance, and in farther illustration of the use of herrings, here
is some account of the maintenance of young painters and lawyers in Edinburgh, sixty years since, sent me by the third Fors, and good Dr Brown, in an

days' work that are properly accounted for in the production.

" How am I to hinder people from giving more if they
like ? "

People whom I catch doing as they like will generally
have to leave the estate.

" But how is it to be decided to which of two pur-
chasers, each willing to give its price, and more, anything
is to belong ? "

In various ways, according to the nature of the thing
sold, and circumstances of sale. Sometimes by priority,
sometimes by privilege ; sometimes by lot, and sometimes by auction, at which whatever excess of price, above
its recorded value, the article brings, shall go to the
national treasury. So that nobody will ever buy anything to make a profit on it.

11*th January*, 1874.—Thinking I should be the better
of a look at the sea, I have come down to an old
watering-place, where one used to be able to get into

admirable sketch of the life of an admirable Scottish artist, says : " Raeburn
(Sir Henry) was left an orphan at six, and was educated in Heriot's Hospital.
At fifteen he was apprenticed to a goldsmith ; but after his time was out, set
himself entirely to portrait painting. About this time he became acquainted
with the famous cynic, lawyer, and wit, John Clerk, afterwards Lord Eldon,
then a young advocate. Both were poor. Young Clerk asked Raeburn to
dine at his lodgings. Coming in, he found the landlady laying the cloth, and
setting down two dishes, one containing three herrings, and the other three
potatoes. 'Is this a'?' said John. Ay, it's a'. 'A'! didna I tell ye,
woman, that a gentleman is to dine wi' me, and that ye were to get six herrin'
and six potatoes ? ' "

a decent little inn, and possess one's self of a parlour
with a bow window looking out on the beach, a pretty
carpet, and a print or two of revenue cutters, and the
Battle of the Nile. One could have a chop and some
good cheese for dinner; fresh cream and cresses for
breakfast, and a plate of shrimps.

I find myself in the Umfraville Hotel, a quarter of a
mile long by a furlong deep; in a ghastly room, five-
and-twenty feet square, and eighteen high,—that is to
say, just four times as big as I want, and which I can
no more light with my candles in the evening than I
could the Peak cavern. A gas apparatus in the middle
of it serves me to knock my head against, but I take
good care not to light it, or I should soon be stopped
from my evening's work by a headache, and be unfit for
my morning's business besides. The carpet is thread-
bare, and has the look of having been spat upon all
over. There is only one window, of four huge panes
of glass, through which one commands a view of a
plaster balcony, some ornamental iron railings, an espla-
nade,—and,—well, I suppose,—in the distance, that is
really the sea, where it used to be. I am ashamed to
ask for shrimps,—not that I suppose I could get any if
I did. There's no cream, " because, except in the season,
we could only take so small a quantity, sir." The
bread's stale, because it's Sunday; and the cheese, last
night, was of the cheapest tallow sort. The bill will be
at least three times my old bill;—I shall get no thanks

from anybody for paying it;—and this is what the modern British public thinks is "living in style." But the most comic part of all the improved arrangements is that I can only have codlings for dinner, because all the cod goes to London, and none of the large fishing-boats dare sell a fish, here.

And now but a word or two more, final, as to the fixed price of this book.

A sensible and worthy tradesman writes to me in very earnest terms of expostulation, blaming me for putting the said book out of the reach of most of the persons it is meant for, and asking me how I can expect, for instance, the working men round him (in Lancashire),—who have been in the habit of strictly ascertaining that they have value for their money,—to buy, for tenpence, what they know might be given them for twopence-halfpenny.

Answer first :

My book is meant for no one who cannot reach it. If a man with all the ingenuity of Lancashire in his brains, and breed of Lancashire in his body, with all the steam and coal power in Lancashire to back his ingenuity and muscle, all the press of literary England vomiting the most valuable information at his feet; with all the tenderness of charitable England aiding him in his efforts, and ministering to his needs, with all the liberality of republican Europe rejoicing in his dignities as a man and a brother, and with all the science of enlightened Europe directing his opinions on the subject

of the materials of the Sun, and the origin of his species ;
if, I say, a man so circumstanced, assisted, and informed,
living besides in the richest country of the globe, and,
from his youth upwards, having been in the habit of
'seeing that he had value for his money,' cannot, as
the upshot and net result of all, now afford to pay me
tenpence a month—or an annual half-sovereign, for my
literary labour,—in Heaven's name, let him buy the best
reading he can for twopence-halfpenny.　For that sum, I
clearly perceive he can at once provide himself with two
penny illustrated newspapers and one halfpenny one,—full
of art, sentiment, and the Tichborne trial.　He can buy a
quarter of the dramatic works of Shakespeare, or a whole
novel of Sir Walter Scott's.　Good value for his money,
he thinks ;—reads one of them through, and in all probability loses some five years of the eyesight of his old age ;
which he does not, with all his Lancashire ingenuity,
reckon as part of the price of his cheap book.　But how
has he read ?　There is an act of Midsummer Night's
Dream printed in a page.　Steadily and dutifully, as a
student should, he reads his page.　The lines slip past
his eyes, and mind, like sand in an hour-glass ; he has
some dim idea at the end of the act that he has been
reading about Fairies, and Flowers, and Asses.　Does
he know what a Fairy is ?　Certainly not.　Does he
know what a flower is ?　He has perhaps never seen
one wild, or happy, in his life　Does he even know—
quite distinctly, inside and out—what an Ass is ?

But, answer second. Whether my Lancashire friends need any aid to their discernment of what is good or bad in literature, I do not know ;—but I mean to give them the best help I can ; and, therefore, not to allow them to have for twopence what I know to be worth tenpence. For here is another law of Florence, still concerning fish, which is transferable at once to literature.

" Eel of the lake shall be sold for three soldi a pound ; and eel of the common sort for a soldo and a half."

And eel of a bad sort was not allowed to be sold at all.

" Eel of the lake," I presume, was that of the Lake of Bolsena ; Pope Martin IV. died of eating too many, in spite of their high price. You observe I do not reckon my Fors Eel to be of Bolsena ; I put it at the modest price of a soldo a pound, or English tenpence. One cannot be precise in such estimates ;—one can only obtain rude approximations. Suppose, for instance, you read the Times newspaper for a week, from end to end ; your aggregate of resultant useful information will certainly not be more than you may get out of a single number of Fors. But your Times for the week will cost you eighteenpence.

You borrow the Times ? Borrow this then ; till the days come when English people cease to think they can live by lending, or learn by borrowing.

I finish with copy of a bit of a private letter to the

editor of an honestly managed country newspaper, who asked me to send him Fors.

"I find it—on examining the subject for these last three years very closely—necessary to defy the entire principle of advertisement ; and to make no concession of any kind whatsoever to the public press—even in the minutest particular.   And this year I cease sending Fors to *any* paper whatsoever.   It *must* be bought by everyone who has it, editor or private person.

"If there are ten people in ————— willing to subscribe a penny each for it, you can see it in turn ; by no other means can I let it be seen.   From friend to friend, or foe to foe, it must make its own way, or stand still, abiding its time."

NOTES AND CORRESPONDENCE.

The following bit of a private letter to a good girl belonging to the upper classes may be generally useful, so I asked her to copy it for Fors.

"*January*, 1874

"Now mind you dress always charmingly; it is the first duty of a girl to be charming, and she cannot be charming if she is not charmingly dressed.

"And it is quite the first of firsts in the duties of girls in high position, nowadays, to set an example of beautiful dress without extravagance,—that is to say, without waste, or unnecessary splendour.

"On great occasions they may be a blaze of jewels, if they like, and can; but only when they are part of a great show or ceremony In their daily life, and ordinary social relations, they ought *at present* to dress with marked simplicity, to put down the curses of luxury and waste which are consuming England.

"Women usually apologize to themselves for their pride and vanity, by saying, ' It is good for trade.'

"Now you may soon convince yourself, and everybody about you, of the monstrous folly of this, by a very simple piece of definite action.

"Wear, yourself, becoming, pleasantly varied, but simple dress, of the best possible material.

" What you think necessary to buy (beyond this) 'for the good of trade,' buy, and immediately *burn*.

" Even your dullest friends will see the folly of that proceeding. You can then explain to them that by wearing what they don't want (instead of burning it) for the good of trade, they are merely adding insolence and vulgarity to absurdity."

I am very grateful to the writer of the following letters for his permission to print the portions of them bearing on our work. The first was written several years ago.

" Now, my dear friend, I don't know why I should intrude what I now want to say about my little farm, which you disloyally dare to call a kingdom, but that I know you *do* feel an interest in such things; whereas I find not one in a hundred does care a jot for the moral influence and responsibilities of landowners, or for those who live out of it, and by the sweat of the brow for them and their own luxuries which pamper them, whilst too often their tenants starve, and the children die of want and fever.

" One of the most awful things I almost ever heard was from the lips of a clergyman, near B——, when asked what became of the children, by day, of those mothers employed in mills. He said, 'Oh, I take care of them; they are brought to me, and I lay them in the churchyard.' Poor lambs! What a flock!

" But now for my little kingdom,—the *royalties* of which, by the way, still go to the Duke of Devonshire, as lord of the minerals under the earth.

" It had for many years been a growing dream and desire of mine (whether right or wrong I do not say) to possess a piece of God's earth, be it only a rock or a few acres of land, with a few people to live out of and upon it. Well, my good father had an estate about four miles across, embracing the whole upper streams and head of ——dale, some twelve hundred feet above the sea, and lifted thus far away above the din and smoke of men, surrounded by higher hills, the grassy slopes of Ingleborough and Carn Fell. It was a waste moorland, with a few sheep farms on it, undivided, held in common,—a few small enclosures of grass and flowers, taken off at the time of the Danes, retaining Danish names and farm usages,—a few tenements, built by that great and noble Lady Anne Clifford, two hundred years ago ; in which dwelt honest, sturdy, great-hearted English men and women, as I think this land knows

"Well, this land my father made over by deed of gift to me, reserving to himself the rents for life, but granting to me full liberty to 'improve' and lay out what I pleased, charged also with the maintenance of a schoolmaster for the little school-house I built in memory of my late wife, who loved the place and people. With this arrangement I was well pleased, and at once began to enclose and drain, and, on Adam Smith principle, make two blades of grass grow where one grew before. This has gone on for some years, affording labour to the few folks there, and some of their neighbours. Of the prejudices of the old farmers, the less said the better, and as to the prospective increased value of rental, I may look, at least, for my five per cent., may I not? I am well repaid, at present, by the delight gained to me in wandering over this little Arcady, where I fancy at times I still hear the strains of the pipe of the shepherd Lord Clifford of Cumberland, blending with the crow of the moor-fowl, the song of the lark, and cry of the curlew, the bleating of sheep, and heaving and dying fall of the many waters To think of all this, and yet men prefer the din of war or commercial strife! It is so pleasant a thing to know all the inhabitants, and all their little joys and woes,—like one of your bishops; and to be able to apportion them their work Labour, there, is not accounted degrading work, even stone-breaking for the roads is not *pauper's* work, and a test of starvation, but taken gladly by tenant farmers to occupy spare time for I at once set to work to make roads, rude bridges, plantations of fir-trees, and of oak and birch, which once flourished there, as the name signifies.

" I am now laying out some thousands of pounds in draining and liming, and *killing out* the Alpine flowers, which you tell me ' is not wrong to do, as God has reserved other gardens for them, though I must say not one dies without a pang to me ; yet I see there springs up the fresh grass, the daisy, the primrose—the life of growing men and women, the source of labour and of happiness , God be thanked if one does even a little to attain that for one's fellows, either for this world or the next !

" How I wish you could see them on our one day's feast and holiday, when all—as many as will come from all the country round—are regaled with a hearty Yorkshire tea at the *Hall*, as they will call a rough mullioned-windowed house I built upon a rock rising from the river's edge.   The children have their games. and then all join in a missionary meeting, to hear something of their fellow-creatures who live in other lands ; the little ones gather their pennies to support and educate a little Indian school child ; † this not only for sentiment, but to teach a care for others near home and far off.

" The place is five miles from church, and, happily, as far from a public-house, though still, I grieve to say, drink is the one failing of these good people, mostly arising from the want of full occupation.

" You speak of *mining* as servile work   why so ?   Hugh Miller was a quarryman, and I know an old man who has wrought coal

* I don't remember telling you anything of the sort.   I should tell you another story now, my dear friend.

† Very fine , but have all the children in Sheffield and Leeds had their pennyworth of gospel, first ?

for me in a narrow seam, lying on his side to work, who has told me that in winter time he had rather work thus than sit over his fireside; * he is quiet and undisturbed, earns his bread, and is a man not without reflection. Then there is the smith, an artist in his way, and loves *his* work too ; and as to the quarrymen and masons, they are some of the merriest fellows I know : they come five or six miles to work, *knitting* stockings as they walk along.

"I must just allude to one social feature which is pleasant,— that is, the free intercourse, without familiarity, or loss of respect for master and man. The farmer or small landowner sits at the same table at meals with the servants, yet the class position of yeoman or labourer is fully maintained, and due respect shown to the superior, and almost royal worship to the lord of the soil, if he is in anywise a good landlord. Now, is England quite beyond all hope, when such things exist here, in this nineteenth century of machine-made life ? I know not why, I say again, I should inflict all this about *self* upon you, except that I have a hobby, and I love it, and so fancy others must do so too.

"Forgive me this, and believe me always,

"Yours affectionately."

"*5th January*, 1874

"My dear Mr Ruskin,—I have just come from an old Tudor house in Leicestershire, which tells of happier days in some ways than our own. It was once the Grange of St. Mary's Abbey, where rent and service were paid and done *in kind* When there, I wished I could have gone a few miles with you to St. Bernard's Monastery in Charnwood Forest; there you

---

* All I can say is, tastes differ , but I have not myself tried the degree of comfort which may be attained in winter by lying on one's side in a coal-seam, and cannot therefore feel confidence in offering an opinion.

would see what somewhat resembles your St. George's land, only without the family and domestic features—certainly most essential to the happiness of a people.*   But there you may see rich well-kept fields and gardens, where thirty years ago was nothing but wild moorland and granite tors on the hill ridges.

" The Cross of Calvary rises now on the highest rock ; below are gardens and fields, all under the care and labour (happy labour it seems) of the Silent Brothers,† and a reformatory for boys.   There is still much waste land adjoining.   The spot is central, healthy, and as yet unoccupied : it really seems to offer itself to you.   There, too, is space, pure air and water, and quarries of slate and granite, etc., for the less skilled labour.

" Well, you ask if the dalesmen of Yorkshire rise to a vivid state of contented life and love of the pretty things of heaven and earth.   They have a rough outside, at times hard to pene-trate ; but when you do, there is a warm heart, but not much culture, although a keen value of manly education, and their duty to God and man.   Apart from the vanities of the so-called ' higher education,' their calling is mostly out of doors, in com-pany with sheep and cattle ; the philosophy of their minds often worthy of the Shepherd Lord,—not much sight for the beauties of Nature beyond its *uses*.   I CAN say their tastes are not *low* nor *degraded* by literature of the daily press, etc.   I have known

* Very much so indeed, my good friend : and yet, the plague of it is, one never can get people to do anything that is wise or generous. unless they go and make monks of themselves   I believe this St. George's land of mine will really be the first place where it has been attempted to get married people to live in any charitable and human way, and graft apples where they may eat them, without getting driven out of their Paradise.

† There, again ! why, in the name of all that's natural, can t decent men and women use their tongues, on occasion, for what God made them for,—talking in a civil way ; but must either go and make dumb beasts of themselves, or else (far worse) let out their tongues for hire, and live by vomiting novels and reviews !

them for twenty years, have stood for hours beside them at work, building or draining, and I never heard one foul or coarse word In sickness, both man and woman are devoted. They have, too, a reverence for social order and 'Divine Law,'—familiar without familiarity. This even pervades their own class or sub-classes, —for instance, although farmers and their families, and work-people and servants, all sit at the same table, it is a rare thing for a labourer to presume to ask in marriage a farmer's daughter Their respect to landlords is equally shown. As a specimen of their politics, I may instance this;—to a man at the county election they voted for Stuart Wortley, 'because he bore a well-known Yorkshire name, and had the blood of a gentle-man.'

"As to *hardships*, I see none beyond those incident to their calling, in snow-storms, etc. You never see a child unshod or ill-clad. Very rarely do they allow a relative to receive aid from the parish.

"I tried a reading club for winter evenings, but found they liked their own fireside better. Happily, there is, in my part, no public-house within six miles; still I must say drink is the vice of some. In winter they have much leisure time, in which there is a good deal of card-playing. Still some like reading, and we have among them now a fair lot of books, mostly from the Pure Literature Society. They are proud and independent, and, as you say, must be dealt with cautiously. Everywhere I see much might be done. Yet on the whole, when compared with the town life of men, one sees little to amend. There is a pleasant and curious combination of work. Mostly all workmen, —builders (*i e* wallers), carpenters, smiths, etc.,—work a little farm as well as follow their own craft, this gives wholesome occupation as well as independence, and almost realizes Sir T. More's Utopian plan. There is contented life of men, women, and children,—happy in their work and joyful in prospect what could one desire further, if each be full according to his capacity and refinement?

" You ask what I purpose to do further, or leave untouched. I desire to leave untouched some 3,000 acres of moorland needed for their sheep, serviceable for peat fuel, freedom of air and mind and body, and the growth of all the lovely things of moss and heather. Wherever land is capable of improvement, I hold it is a grave responsibility until it is done. You must come and look for yourself some day.

" I enclose a cheque for ten guineas for St. George's Fund, with my best wishes for this new year.

" Ever yours affectionately."

I have questioned one or two minor points in my friend's letters, but on the whole, they simply describe a piece of St George's old England, still mercifully left,—and such as I hope to make even a few pieces more, again; conquering them out of the Devil's new England.

FORS CLAVIGERA.

LETTER THE 39th.

THE CART GOES BETTER, SO

ON a foggy forenoon, two or three days ago, I wanted to make my way quickly from Hengler's Circus to Drury Lane Theatre, without losing time which might be philosophically employed ; and therefore afoot, for in a cab I never can think of anything but how the driver is to get past whatever is in front of him.

On foot, then, I proceeded, and accordingly by a somewhat complex diagonal line, to be struck, as the stars might guide me, between Regent Circus and Covent Garden. I have never been able, by the way, to make any coachman understand that such diagonals were not always profitable. Coachmen, as far as I know them, always possess just enough geometry to feel that the hypothenuse is shorter than the two sides, but I never yet could get one to see that an hypothenuse constructed of cross streets in the manner of the line A C, had no advantage, in the matter of distance to be traversed, over the simple thoroughfares A B, B C, while it involved the loss of the momentum of the carriage, and a fresh

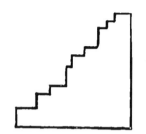 start for the cattle, at seventeen corners instead of one, not to mention the probability of a block at half a dozen of them, none the less frequent since underground railways, and more difficult to get out of, in consequence of the increasing discourtesy and diminishing patience of all human creatures.

Now here is just one of the pieces of practical geometry and dynamics which a modern schoolmaster, exercising his pupils on the positions of letters in the word Chillian-wallah, would wholly despise. Whereas, in St. George's schools, it shall be very early learned, on a square and diagonal of actual road, with actual loaded wheelbarrow—first one-wheeled, and pushed ; and secondly, two-wheeled, and pulled. And similarly, every bit of science the children learn shall be directly applied by them, and the use of it felt, which involves the truth of it being known in the best possible way, and without any debating thereof. And what they cannot apply they shall not be troubled to know. I am not the least desirous that they should know so much even of the sun as that it stands still, (if it does) They may remain, for anything I care, under the most simple conviction that it gets up every morning and goes to bed every night ; but they shall assuredly possess the applicable science of the hour it gets up at, and goes to bed at, on any day of the year, because they will have to regulate their own gettings up and goings to bed upon those solar proceedings

Well, to return to Regent Street. Being afoot, I took the complex diagonal, because by wise regulation of one's time and angle of crossing, one may indeed move on foot in an economically drawn line, provided one does not miss its main direction. As it chanced, I took my line correctly enough ; but found so much to look at and think of on the way, that I gained no material advantage First, I could not help stopping to consider the metaphysical reasons of the extreme gravity and self-abstraction of Archer Street. Then I was delayed a while in Prince's Street, Soho, wondering what Prince it had belonged to. Then I got through Gerrard Street into Little Newport Street , and came there to a dead pause, to think why, in these days of division of mechanical labour, there should be so little space for classification of commodities, as to require oranges, celery, butchers' meat, cheap hosiery, soap, and salt fish, to be all sold in the same alley.

Some clue to the business was afforded me by the sign of the ' Hotel de l'Union des Peuples ' at the corner, " bouillon et bœuf à emporter , " but I could not make out why, in spite of the union of people, the provision merchant at the opposite corner had given up business, and left his house with all its upper windows broken, and its door nailed up. Finally, I was stopped at the corner of Cranbourne Street by a sign over a large shop advising me to buy some " screwed boots and shoes." I am too shy

to go in and ask, on such occasions, what screwed boots
are, or at least too shy to come cut again without buying
any, if the people tell me politely, and yet I couldn't get
the question what such things may be out of my head, and
nearly got run over in consequence, before attaining the
Arcadian shelter of Covent Garden. I was but just in
time to get my tickets for Jack in the Box, on the day
I wanted, and put them carefully in the envelope with
those I had been just securing at Hengler's for my fifth
visit to Cinderella. For indeed, during the last three
weeks, the greater part of my available leisure has been
spent between Cinderella and Jack in the box ; with this
curious result upon my mind, that the intermediate scenes
of Archer Street and Prince's Street, Soho, have become
to me merely as one part of the drama, or pantomime,
which I happen to have seen last ; or, so far as the difference in the appearance of men and things may compel me
to admit some kind of specific distinction, I begin to ask
myself, Which is the reality, and which the pantomime ?
Nay, it appears to me not of much moment which we
choose to call Reality. Both are equally real ; and the
only question is whether the cheerful state of things which
the spectators, especially the youngest and wisest, entirely
applaud and approve at Hengler's and Drury Lane, must
necessarily be interrupted always by the woful interlude
of the outside world.

It is a bitter question to me, for I am myself now,
hopelessly, a man of the world !—of that woful outside

one, I mean. It is now Sunday ; half-past eleven in the morning. Everybody about me is gone to church except the kind cook, who is straining a point of conscience to provide me with dinner. Everybody else is gone to church, to ask to be made angels of, and profess that they despise the world and the flesh, which I find myself always living in, (rather, perhaps, living, or endeavouring to live, in too little of the last). And I am left alone with the cat, in the world of sin.

But I scarcely feel less an outcast when I come out of the Circus, on week days, into my own world of sorrow. Inside the Circus, there have been wonderful Mr. Edward Cooke, and pretty Mademoiselle Aguzzi, and the three brothers Leonard, like the three brothers in a German story, and grave little Sandy, and bright and graceful Miss Hengler, all doing the most splendid feats of strength, and patience, and skill. There have been dear little Cinderella and her Prince, and all the pretty children beautifully dressed, taught thoroughly how to behave, and how to dance, and how to sit still, and giving everybody delight that looks at them ; whereas, the instant I come outside the door, I find all the children about the streets ill-dressed, and ill-taught, and ill-behaved, and nobody cares to look at them. And then, at Drury Lane, there's just everything I want people to have always, got for them, for a little while ; and they seem to enjoy them just as I should expect they would. Mushroom Common, with its lovely mushrooms, white and gray, so finely set off by the

incognita fairy's scarlet cloak ; the golden land of plenty
with furrow and sheath, Buttercup Green, with its flock of
mechanical sheep, which the whole audience claps because
they are of pasteboard, as they do the sheep in Little
Red Riding Hood because they are alive, but in either
case, must have them on the stage in order to be pleased
with them, and never clap when they see the creatures in a
field outside   They can't have enough, any more than I
can, of the loving duet between Tom Tucker and little Bo
Peep· they would make the dark fairy dance all night
long in her amber light if they could ; and yet contentedly
return to what they call a necessary state of things outside,
where their corn is reaped by machinery, and the only
duets are between steam whistles.   Why haven't they a
steam whistle to whistle to them on the stage, instead
of Miss Violet Cameron ?   Why haven't they a steam
Jack in the Box to jump for them, instead of Mr.
Evans ? or a steam doll to dance for them, instead of
Miss Kate Vaughan ?   They still seem to have human
ears and eyes, in the Theatre ; to know *there*, for an
hour or two, that golden light, and song, and human
skill and grace, are better than smoke-blackness, and
shrieks of iron and fire, and monstrous powers of constrained elements.   And then they return to their
underground railroad, and say, 'This, behold,—this is
the right way to move, and live in a real world'

Very notable it is also that just as in these two
theatrical entertainments—the Church and the Circus,

—the imaginative congregations still retain some true notions of the value of human and beautiful things, and don't have steam-preachers nor steam-dancers,—so also they retain some just notion of the truth, in moral things: Little Cinderella, for instance, at Hengler's, never thinks of offering her poor fairy Godmother a ticket from the Mendicity Society. She immediately goes and fetches her some dinner. And she makes herself generally useful, and sweeps the doorstep, and dusts the door;—and none of the audience think any the worse of her on that account. They think the worse of her proud sisters who make her do it But when they leave the Circus, they never think for a moment of making *themselves* useful, like Cinderella. They forthwith play the proud sisters as much as they can; and try to make anybody else, who will, sweep their doorsteps Also, at Hengler's, nobody advises Cinderella to write novels, instead of doing her washing, by way of bettering herself. The audience, gentle and simple, feel that the only chance she has of pleasing her Godmother, or marrying a prince, is in remaining patiently at her tub, as long as the Fates will have it so, heavy though it be. Again, in all dramatic representation of Little Red Riding Hood, everybody disapproves of the carnivorous propensities of the Wolf. They clearly distinguish there—as clearly as the Fourteenth Psalm, itself—between the class of animal which eats, and

the class of animal which is eaten. But once outside the theatre, they declare the whole human race
to be universally carnivorous—and are ready themselves to eat up any quantity of Red Riding
Hoods, body and soul, if they can make money by
them.

And lastly,—at Hengler's and Drury Lane, see how
the whole of the pleasure of life depends on the
existence of Princes, Princesses, and Fairies. One never
hears of a Republican pantomime; one never thinks
Cinderella would be a bit better off if there were no
princes. The audience understand that though it is
not every good little housemaid who can marry a
prince, the world would not be the least pleasanter,
for the rest, if there were no princes to marry.

Nevertheless, it being too certain that the sweeping
of doorsteps diligently will not in all cases enable a
pretty maiden to drive away from said doorsteps, for
evermore, in a gilded coach,—one has to consider what
may be the next best for her. And next best, or, in
the greater number of cases, best altogether, will be
that Love, with his felicities, should himself enter over
the swept and garnished steps, and abide with her in
her own life, such as it is. And since St. Valentine's
grace is with us, at this season, I will finish my Fors,
for this time, by carrying on our little romance of the
Broom-maker, to the place in which he unexpectedly
finds it. In which romance, while we may perceive the

principal lesson intended by the author to be that the delights and prides of affectionate married life are consistent with the humblest station, (or may even be more easily found there than in a higher one,) we may for ourselves draw some farther conclusions which the good Swiss pastor only in part intended. We may consider in what degree the lightening of the wheels of Hansli's cart, when they drave heavily by the wood of Muri, corresponds to the change of the English highway into Mount Parnassus, for Sir Philip Sidney ; and if the correspondence be not complete, and some deficiency in the divinest power of Love be traceable in the mind of the simple person as compared to that of the gentle one, we may farther consider, in due time, how, without help from any fairy Godmother, we may make Cinderella's life gentle to her, as well as simple ; and, without taking the peasant's hand from his labour, make his heart leap with joy as pure as a king's.*

Well, said Hansli, I'll help you, give me your bag, I'll put it among my brooms, and nobody will see it. Everybody knows *me* Not a soul will think I've got your shoes underneath there You've only to tell me where to leave them—or indeed where to stop for you,

---

* If to any reader, looking back on the history of Europe for the last four centuries, this sentence seems ironical, let him be assured that for the causes which make it seem so, during the last four centuries the end of kinghood has come.

if you like. You can follow a little way off ;—nobody will think we have anything to do with each other.

The young girl made no compliments.*

You are really very good, † said she, with a more serene face. She brought her packet, and Hans hid it so nicely that a cat couldn't have seen it.

Shall I push, or help you to pull ? asked the young girl, as if it had been a matter of course that she should also do her part in the work.

As you like best, though you needn't mind ; it isn't a pair or two of shoes that will make my cart much heavier. The young girl began by pushing ; but that did not last long. Presently she found herself ‡ in front, pulling also by the pole.

It seems to me that the cart goes better so, said she. As one ought to suppose, she pulled with all her strength ; that which nevertheless did not put her out of breath, nor hinder her from relating all she had in her head, or heart.

* Untranslateable. It means, she made no false pretence of reluctance, and neither politely nor feebly declined what she meant to accept. But the phrase might be used of a person accepting with ungraceful eagerness, or want of sense of obligation. A slight sense of this simplicity is meant by our author to be here included in the expression.

† "Trop bon." It is a little more than 'very good,' but not at all equivalent to our English 'too good.'

‡ "Se trouva." Untranslateable. It is very little more than 'was' in front. But that little more,—the slight sense of not knowing quite how she got there,- is necessary to mark the under-current of meaning ; she goes behind the cart first, thinking it more modest , but presently, nevertheless, 'finds herself' in front ; "the cart goes better, so."

They got to the top of the hill of Stalden without Hansli's knowing how that had happened: the long alley * seemed to have shortened itself by half.

There, one made one's dispositions, the young girl stopped behind, while Hansli, with her bag and his brooms, entered the town without the least difficulty, where he remitted her packet to the young girl, also without any accident, but they had scarcely time to say a word to each other before the press † of people, cattle, and vehicles separated them. Hansli had to look after his cart, lest it should be knocked to bits And so ended the acquaintanceship for that day. This vexed Hansli not a little, howbeit he didn't think long about it. We cannot (more's the pity) affirm that the young girl had made an ineffaceable impression upon him,—and all the less, that she was not altogether made for producing ineffaceable impressions. She was a stunted little girl, with a broad face. That which, she had of best was a good heart, and an indefatigable ardour for work; but those are things which, externally, are not very remarkable, and many people don't take much notice of them.

Nevertheless, the next Tuesday, when Hansli saw himself‡ at his cart again, he found it extremely heavy

---

* There used to be an avenue of tall trees, about a quarter of a mile long, on the Thun road, just at the brow of the descent to the bridge of the Aar, at the lower end of the main street of Berne.

† "Cohue." Confused and moving mass We have no such useful word.

‡ "Se revit" It would not be right to say here 'se trouva,' because

I wouldn't have believed, said he to himself, what a difference there is between two pulling, and one.

Will she be there again, I wonder, thought he, as he came near the little wood of Muri. I would take her bag very willingly if she would help me to pull. Also the road is nowhere so ugly as between here and the town.*

And behold that it precisely happened that the young girl was sitting there upon the same bench, all the same as eight days before ; only with the difference that she was not crying.

Have you got anything for me to carry to-day ? asked Hansli, who found his cart at once became a great deal lighter at the sight of the young girl.

It is not only for that that I have waited, answered she ; even if I had had nothing to carry to the town, I should have come, all the same ; for eight days ago I wasn't able to thank you ; nor to ask if that cost any-thing.

A fine question ! said Hansli. Why, you served me for a second donkey, and yet I never asked how much

there is no surprise, or discovery, in the doing once again what is done every week. But one may nevertheless contemplate oneself, and the situation, from a new point of view. Hansli 'se revit'—reviewed himself, literally ; a very proper operation, every now and then for everybody.

* A slight difference between the Swiss and English peasant is marked here, to the advantage of the former. At least, I imagine an English Hansli would not have known, even in love, whether the road was ugly or pretty.

I owed you for helping me to pull! So, as all that went of itself, the young girl brought her bundle, and Hansli hid it, and she went to put herself at the pole as if she had known it all by heart. I had got a little way from home, said she, before it came into my head that I ought to have brought a cord to tie to the cart behind, and that would have gone better; but another time, if I return, I won't forget.

This association for mutual help found itself, then, established, without any longer diplomatic debates, and in the most simple manner. And, that day, it chanced that they were also able to come back together as far as the place where their roads parted; all the same, they were so prudent as not to show themselves together before the gens-d'armes at the town gates.

And now for some time Hansli's mother had been quite enchanted with her son. It seemed to her he was more gay, she said. He whistled and sang, now, all the blessed day, and tricked himself up, so that he could never have done.* Only just the other day he had bought a great-coat of drugget, in which he had nearly the air of a real counsellor. But she could not find any fault with him for all that, he was so good to her that certainly the good God must reward him,—as for herself, she was in no way of doing it, but could do nothing but pray for him. Not that you are to think, said she, that he puts everything into his clothes,

---

* "Se requinquait a n'en plus finir.' Entirely beyond English rendering.

he has some money too. If God spares his life, I'll wager that one day he'll come to have a cow :—he has been talking of a goat ever so long ; but it's not likely I shall be spared to see it. And, after all, I don't pretend to be sure it will ever be.

Mother, said Hans one day, I don't know how it is ; but either the cart gets heavier, or I'm not so strong as I was ; for some time I've scarcely been able to manage it. It is getting really too much for me ; especially on the Berne road, where there are so many hills.

I dare say, said the mother ; aussi, why do you go on loading it more every day ? I've been fretting about you many a time ; for one always suffers for over-work when one gets old. But you must take care. Put a dozen or two of brooms less on it, and it will roll again all right.

That's impossible, mother ; I never have enough as it is, and I haven't time to go to Berne twice a week.

But, Hansli, suppose you got a donkey. I've heard say they are the most convenient beasts in the world ᐧ they cost almost nothing, eat almost nothing, and any-thing one likes to give them ; and that's * as strong as a horse, without counting that one can make something

* " Ça." Note the peculiar character and value, in modern French, of this general and slightly depreciatory pronoun, essentially a republican word,—hurried, inconsiderate, and insolent. The popular chant ' ça ira' gives the typical power.

of the milk,—not that I want any, but one may speak of it.*

No, . mother, said Hansli,—they're as self-willed as devils : sometimes one can't get them to do anything at all ; and then what I should do with a donkey the other five days of the week ! No, mother ;—I was thinking of a wife,—hey, what say you ?

But, Hansli, I think a goat or a donkey would be much better. A wife ! What sort of idea is that that has come into your head ? What would you do with a wife ?

Do ! said Hansli ; what other people do, I suppose ; and then, I thought she would help me to draw the cart, which goes ever so much better with another hand : —without counting that she could plant potatoes between times, and help me to make my brooms, which I couldn't get a goat or a donkey to do.

But, Hansli, do you think to find one, then, who will help you to draw the cart, and will be clever enough to do all that ? asked the mother, searchingly.

Oh, mother, there's one who has helped me already often with the cart, said Hansli, and who would be good for a great deal besides ; but as to whether she would marry me or not, I don't know, for I haven't asked her. I thought that I would tell you first.

You rogue of a boy, what's that you tell me there ?

---

* " C'est seulement pour dire." I've been at least ten minutes trying to translate it, and can't.

I don't understand a word of it, cried the mother. You too!—are you also like that? The good God Himself might have told me, and I wouldn't have believed Him. What's that you say?—you've got a girl to help you to pull the cart! A pretty business to engage her for! Ah well,—trust men after this!

Thereupon Hansli put himself to recount the history; and how that had happened quite by chance; and how that girl was just expressly made for him: a girl as neat as a clock,—not showy, not extravagant,—and who would draw the cart better even than a cow could. But I haven't spoken to her of anything, however. All the same, I think I'm not disagreeable to her. Indeed, she has said to me once or twice that she wasn't in a hurry to marry, but if she could manage it, so as not to be worse off than she was now, she wouldn't be long making up her mind She knows, for that matter, very well also why she is in the world. Her little brothers and sisters are growing up after her, and she knows well how things go, and how the youngest are always made the most of, for one never thinks of thanking the elder ones for the trouble they've had in bringing them up.

All that didn't much displease the mother, and the more she ruminated over these unexpected matters, the more it all seemed to her very proper Then she put herself to make inquiries, and learned that nobody knew the least harm of the girl. They told her she did all she could to help her parents ; but that with the best they could do, there wouldn't be much to fish for Ah, well : it's all the better, thought she ; for then neither of them can have much to say to the other.

The next Tuesday, while Hansli was getting his cart ready, his mother said to him,

Well, speak to that girl : if she consents, so will I ; but I can't run after her. Tell her to come here on Sunday, that I may see her, and at least we can talk a little. If she is willing to be nice, it will all go very well Aussi, it must happen some time or other, I suppose.

But, mother, it isn't written anywhere that it must happen, whether or no ; and if it doesn't suit you, nothing hinders me from leaving it all alone.

Nonsense, child, don't be a goose. Hasten thee to set out ; and say to that girl, that if she likes to be my daughter-in-law, I'll take her, and be very well pleased.

Hansli set out, and found the young girl. Once that they were pulling together, he at his pole, and she at her cord, Hansli put himself to say,

That certainly goes as quick again when there are thus two cattle at the same cart. Last Saturday I went to Thun by myself, and dragged all the breath out of my body.

Yes, I've often thought, said the young girl, that it was very foolish of you not to get somebody to help you ; all the business would go twice as easily, and you would gain twice as much.

What would you have ? said Hansli. Sometimes one thinks too soon of a thing, sometimes too late,—one's always mortal.* But now it really seems to me that I should like to have somebody for a help ; if you were of the same mind, you would be just the good thing for me. If that suits you, I'll marry you.

Well, why not,—if you don't think me too ugly nor too poor ? answered the young girl. Once you've got me, it will be too late to despise me. As for me, I could scarcely fall in with a better chance. One always gets a husband,—but, aussi, of what sort ? You are quite good enough † for me : you take care of your affairs, and I don't think you'll treat a wife like a dog.

My faith, she will be as much master as I ; if she is not pleased that way, I don't know what more to do, said Hansli. And for other matters, I don't think you'll be worse off with me than you have been at home. If that suits you, come to see us on Sunday. It's my mother who told me to ask you, and to say that if you liked to be her daughter-in-law, she would be very well pleased.

---

* "On est toujours homme." The proverb is frequent among the French and Germans. The modesty of it is not altogether easy to an English mind, and would be totally incomprehensible to an ordinary Scotch one.

† "Assez brave." Untranslateable, except by the old English sense of the word brave, and even that has more reference to outside show than the French word.

Liked ! But what could I want more ! I am used to submit myself, and take things as they come,—worse to-day, better to-morrow,—sometimes more sour, sometimes less I never have thought that a hard word made a hole in me, else by this time I shouldn't have had a bit of skin left as big as a kreutzer. But, all the same, I must tell my people, as the custom is. For the rest, they won't give themselves any trouble about the matter. There are enough of us in the house : if any one likes to go, nobody will stop them.*

And, aussi, that was what happened. On Sunday the young girl really appeared at Rychiswyl. Hansli had given her very clear directions , nor had she to ask long before she was told where the broom-seller lived. The mother made her pass a good examination upon the garden and the kitchen ; and would know what book of prayers she used, and whether she could read in the New Testament, and also in the Bible,† for it was very bad for the children, and it was always they who suffered, if the mother didn't know enough for that, said the old woman The girl pleased her, and the affair was concluded.

---

* You are to note carefully the conditions of sentiment in family relationships implied both here, and in the bride's reference, farther on. to her godmother's children. Poverty, with St Francis' pardon, is not always holy in its influence yet a richer girl might have felt exactly the same without being innocent enough to say so.

† I believe the reverend and excellent novelist would himself authorize the distinction , but Hansli's mother must be answerable for it to my Evangelical readers.

You won't have a beauty there, said she to Hansli,
before the young girl; nor much to crow about, in
what she has got. But all that is of no consequence.
It isn't beauty that makes the pot boil; and as for
money, there's many a man who wouldn't marry a girl
unless she was rich, who has had to pay his father-in-
law's debts in the end. When one has health, and work,
in one's arms, one gets along always. I suppose (turning to the girl) you have got two good chemises and
two gowns, so that you won't be the same on Sunday
and work-days?

Oh yes, said the young girl; you needn't give yourself any trouble about that. I've one chemise quite
new, and two good ones besides,—and four others
which, in truth, are rather ragged. But my mother said
I should have another; and my father, that he would
make me my wedding shoes, and they should cost me
nothing. And with that I've a very nice godmother,
who is sure to give me something fine;—perhaps a
saucepan, or a frying-stove,*—who knows? without
counting that perhaps I shall inherit something from
her some day. She has some children, indeed, but they
may die.

Perfectly satisfied on both sides, but especially the
girl, to whom Hansli's house, so perfectly kept in order,
appeared a palace in comparison with her own home,
full of children and scraps of leather, they separated,

* " Poêle à frire ' I don't quite understand the nature of this article.

soon to meet again and quit each other no more. As no soul made the slightest objection, and the preparations were easy,—seeing that new shoes and a new chemise are soon stitched together,—within a month, Hansli was no more alone on his way to Thun. And the old cart went again as well as ever.

And they lived happily ever after? You shall hear The story is not at an end ; note only, in the present phase of it, this most important point, that Hansli does not think of his wife as an expensive luxury, to be refused to himself unless under irresistible temptation. It is only the modern Pall-Mall-pattern Englishman who must 'abstain from the luxury of marriage' if he be wise. Hansli thinks of his wife, on the contrary, as a useful article, which he cannot any longer get on without. He gives us, in fact, a final definition of proper wifely quality,—-" She will draw the cart better than a cow could."

FORS CLAVIGERA.

LETTER THE 40th.

THE SCOTTISH FIRESIDE

I AM obliged to go to Italy this spring, and find beside me, a mass of Fors material in arrear, needing various explanation and arrangement, for which I have no time. Fors herself must look to it, and my readers use their own wits in thinking over what she has looked to. I begin with a piece of Marmontel, which was meant to follow, 'in due time,' the twenty-first letter,—of which, please glance at the last four pages again. This following bit is from another story professing to give some account of Molière's Misanthrope, in his country life, after his last quarrel with Celimène. He calls on a country gentleman, M. de Laval, "and was received by him with the simple and serious courtesy which announces neither the need nor the vain desire of making new connections. Behold, said he, a man who does not surrender himself at once. I esteem him the more. He congratulated M. de Laval on the agreeableness of his solitude　You come to live here, he said to him, far from men, and you are very right to avoid them

I, Monsieur ! I do not avoid men ; I am neither so weak as to fear them, so proud as to despise them, nor so unhappy as to hate them.

This answer struck so home that Alceste was disconcerted by it ; but he wished to sustain his debût, and began to satirize the world

I have lived in the world like another, said M. de Laval, and I have not seen that it was so wicked. There are vices and virtues in it,—good and evil mingled, —I confess ; but nature is so made, and one should know how to accommodate oneself to it.

On my word, said Alceste, in that unison the evil governs to such a point that it chokes the other. Sir, replied the Viscount, if one were as eager to discover good as evil, and had the same delight in spreading the report of it,—if good examples were made public as the bad ones almost always are,—do you not think that the good would weigh down the balance ?* But gratitude speaks so low, and indignation so loudly, that you cannot hear but the last. Both friendship and esteem are commonly moderate in their praises ; they imitate the modesty of honour, in praise, while

---

* Well said, the Viscount. People think me a grumbler ; but I wholly believe this,—nay, *know* this　The world exists, indeed, only by the strength of its silent virtue.

resentment and mortification exaggerate everything they describe.

Monsieur, said Alceste to the Viscount, you make me desire to think as you do, and even if the sad truth were on my side, your error would be preferable. Ah, yes, without doubt, replied M de Laval, ill-humour is good for nothing, the fine part that it is, for a man to play, to fall into a fit of spite like a child!—and why ? For the mistakes of the circle in which one has lived, as if the whole of nature were in the plot against us, and responsible for the hurt we have received.

You are right, replied Alceste, it would be unjust to consider all men as partners in fault; yet how many complaints may we not justly lodge against them, as a body ? Believe me, sir, my judgment of them has serious and grave motives. You will do me justice when you know me. Permit me to see you often! *Often*, said the Viscount, will be difficult. I have much business, and my daughter and I have our studies, which leave us little leisure ; but sometimes, if you will, let us profit by our neighbourhood, at our ease, and without formality, for the privilege of the country is to be alone, when we like.

Some days afterwards Monsieur de Laval returned his visit, and Alceste spoke to him of the pleasure that he doubtless felt in making so many people happy. It is a beautiful example, he said, and, to the shame of men, a very rare one How many persons there are, more power-

ful and more rich than you, who are nothing but a burden
to their inferiors!   I neither excuse nor blame them altogether, replied M. de Laval   In order to do good, one
must know how to set about it, and do not think that it is
so easy to effect our purpose   It is not enough even to be
sagacious, it is needful also to be fortunate, it is necessary
to find sensible and docile persons to manage : * and one
has constantly need of much address, and patience, to lead
the people, naturally suspicious and timid, to what is really
for their advantage.   Indeed, said Alceste, such excuses
are continually made ; but have you not conquered all
these obstacles? and why should not others conquer them?
I, said M. de Laval, have been tempted by opportunity,
and seconded by accident.†   The people of this province,
at the time that I came into possession of my estate, were
in a condition of extreme distress   I did but stretch my
arms to them ; they gave themselves up to me in despair.
An arbitrary tax had been lately imposed upon them,
which they regarded with so much terror that they pre-
ferred sustaining hardships to making any appearance of
having wealth ; and I found, current through the country,
this desolating and destructive maxim, 'The more we
work, the more we shall be trodden down.' "   (It is

---

* Well said, Viscount, again !   So few people know the power of the
Third Fors   If I had not chanced to give lessons in drawing to Octavia
Hill, I could have done nothing in Marylebone, nor she either, for a while
yet, I fancy

† A lovely, classic, unbetterable sentence of Marmontel's, perfect in
wisdom and modesty.

precisely so in England to-day, also.) " *The men dared not be laborious ; the women trembled to have children.*

I went back to the source of the evil. I addressed myself to the man appointed for the reception of the tribute. Monsieur, I said to him, my vassals groan under the weight of the severe measures necessary to make them pay the tax. I wish to hear no more of them ; tell me what is wanting yet to make up the payment for the year, and I will acquit the debt myself. Monsieur, replied the receiver, that cannot be. Why not ? said I. Because it is not the rule. What ! is it not the rule to pay the King the tribute that he demands with the least expense and the least delay possible ? Yes, answered he, that would be enough for the King, but it would not be enough for *me*. Where should *I* be if they paid money down ? It is by the expense of the compulsory measures that I live ; they are the perquisites of my office. To this excellent reason I had nothing to reply, but I went to see the head of the department, and obtained from him the place of receiver-general for my peasants.

My children, I then said to them, (assembling them on my return home,) I have to announce to you that you are in future to deposit in my hands the exact amount of the King's tribute, and no more. There will be no more expenses, no more bailiff's visits. Every Sunday at the bank of the parish, your wives shall bring me their savings, and insensibly you shall find yourselves out of debt. Work now, and cultivate your land ; make the most of it.

you can ; no farther tax shall be laid on you. I answer
for this to you—I who am your father. For those who
are in arrear, I will take some measures for support, or I
will advance them the sum necessary,* and a few days at
the dead time of the year, employed in work for me, will
reimburse me for my expenses. This plan was agreed
upon, and we have followed it ever since. The house-
wives of the village bring me their little offerings : I
encourage them, and speak to them of our good King ;
and what was an act of distressing servitude, has become
an unoppressive act of love.

Finally, as there was a good deal of superfluous time, I
established the workshop that you have seen ; it turns
everything to account, and brings into useful service time
which would be lost between the operations of agriculture : the profits of it are applied to public works. A
still more precious advantage of this establishment is its
having greatly increased the population—more children
are born, as there is certainty of extended means for their
support."

Now note, first, in this passage what material of
loyalty and affection there was still in the French
heart before the Revolution ; and, secondly, how useless
it is to be a good King, if the good King allows his
officers to live upon the cost of compulsory measures.†

* Not for a dividend upon it, I beg you to observe, and even the capital
to be repaid in work.

† Or, worse still, as *our* public men do, upon the cost of *non*-compulsory
measures !

And remember that the French Revolution was the revolt of absolute loyalty and love against the senseless cruelty of a " good King."

Next, for a little specimen of the state of our own working population ; and the "compulsory—not measures, but measureless license," under which their loyalty and love are placed,—here is a genuine working woman's letter ; and if the reader thinks I have given it him in its own spelling that he may laugh at it, the reader is wrong.

"*May* 12, 1873.

" Dear ——

" While Reading the herald to Day on the subject on shortor houers of Labou^r * I was Reminded of A cercomstanc^e that came under my hone notis when the 10 hours sistom Began in the cotton mills in Lancashire I was Minding a mesheen with 30 treds in it I was then maid to mind 2 of 30 treds each with one shillng Advance of wages wich was 5^s for one and 6^s for tow with an increes of speed and with improved mecheens in A few years I was minding tow mecheens with tow 100 trads Each and Dubel speed for 9^s perweek so that in our improved condation we had to turn out some 100 weght per day and we went as if the Devel was After us for 10 houers per day and with that comparetive small Advance in money and the feemals have

* These small " powers " of terminal letters in some of the words are very curious.

ofton Been carred out fainting what with the heat and
hard work and those that could not keep up mst go
and make room for a nother and all this is Done in
Christian England and then we are tould to Be content
in the station of Life in wich the Lord as places us
But I say the Lord never Did place us there so we
have no Right to Be content ₒ that Right and not might
was the Law　yours truely C. H. S."

Next to this account of Machine-labour, here is one
of Hand-labour, also in a genuine letter,—this second
being to myself ; (I wish the other had been also, but it
was to one of my friends).

"Beckenham, Kent,
"*Sept* 24, 1873

"That is a pleasant evening in our family when we
read and discuss the subjects of 'Fors Clavigera,' and
we frequently reperuse them, as for instance, within
a few days, your August letter. In page 16 I was
much struck by the notice of the now exploded use of
the spinning wheel　My mother, a Cumberland woman,
was a spinner, and the whole process, from the fine
thread that passed through her notable fingers, and the
weaving into linen by an old cottager—a very 'Silas
Marner,'—to the bleaching on the orchard grass, was
well known to my sister* and myself, when children.

"When I married, part of the linen that I took to

* A lady high in the ranks of kindly English literature.

my new home was my mother's spinning, and one fine table-cloth was my grandmother's. *What factory, with its thousand spindles, and chemical bleaching powders, can send out such linen as that, which lasted three generations ?* *

"I should not have troubled you with these remarks, had I not at the moment whe n I read your paragraph on hand-spinning, received a letter from my daughter, now for a time resident in Coburg, (a friend of Octavia Hill's,) which bears immediately on the subject. I have therefore ventured to transcribe it for your perusal, believing that the picture she draws from life, beautiful as it is for its simplicity, may give you a moment's pleasure."

"COBURG, *Sept.* 4, 1873

"On Thursday I went to call on Frau L. ; she was not in ; so I went to her mother's, Frau E., knowing that I should find her there. They were all sitting down to afternoon coffee, and asked me to join them, which I gladly did. I had my work-basket with me, and as they were all at work, it was pleasant to do the same thing. Hildigard was there ; in fact she lives there, to take care of Frau E. since she had her fall and stiffened her ankle, a year ago. Hildigard took her spinning, and tied on her white apron, filled the little brass basin of the spinning-wheel with water, to wet her fingers, and set the wheel a-purring. I have never seen

---

* Italics mine, as usual.

the process before, and it was very pretty to see her, with her white fingers, and to hear the little low sound. It is quite a pity, I think, ladies do not do it in England,—it is so pretty, and far nicer work than crochet, and so on, when it is finished. *This soft linen made by hand is so superior to any that you get now.* Presently the four children came in, and the great hunting dog, Feldman, and altogether I thought, as dear little Frau E. sat sewing in her arm-chair, and her old sister near her at her knitting, and Hildigard at her spinning, while pretty Frau L sewed at her little girl's stuff-skirt,—all in the old-fashioned room full of old furniture, and hung round with miniatures of still older dames and officers, in, to our eyes, strange stiff costumes, that it was a most charming scene, and one I enjoyed as much as going to the theatre,—which I did in the evening."

A most charming scene, my dear lady, I have no doubt; just what Hengler's Circus was, to me, this Christmas. Now for a little more of the charming scenery outside, and far away.

" 12, TUNSTALL TERRACE, SUNDERLAND.
" 14*th Feb* 1874.

"My dear Sir,—The rice famine is down upon us in earnest, and finds our wretched 'administration' unprepared—a ministration unto death!

" It can carry childish gossip ' by return of post ' into

every village in India, but not food ; no, not food even for mothers and babes. So far has our scientific and industrial progress attained.

"To-night comes news that hundreds of deaths from starvation have already occurred, and that even high-caste women are working on the roads ;—no food from stores of ours except at the price of degrading, health-destroying, and perfectly useless toil. God help the nation responsible for this wickedness.

"Dear Mr Ruskin, you wield the most powerful pen in England, can you not shame us into some sense of duty, some semblance of human feeling ? [Certainly not. My good sir, as far as I know, nobody ever minds a word I say, except a few nice girls, who are a great comfort to me, but can't do anything. They don't even know how to spin, poor little lilies !]

"I observe that the 'Daily News' of to-day is horrified at the idea that Disraeli should dream of appropriating any part of the surplus revenue to the help of India in this calamity [of course], and even the 'Spectator' calls that a 'dangerous' policy. So far is even 'the conscience of the Press' [What next ?] corrupted by the dismal science.

"I am, yours truly."

So far the Third Fors has arranged matters for me ; but I must put a stitch or two into her work.

Look back to my third letter, for March, 1871, page 5. You see it is said there that the French war and its issues were none of Napoleon's doing, nor Count Bismarck's ; that the mischief in them was St. Louis's doing ; and the good, such as it was, the rough father of Frederick the Great's doing.

The father of Frederick the Great was an Evangelical divine of the strictest orthodoxy,—very fond of beer, bacon, and tobacco, and entirely resolved to have his own way, supposing, as pure Evangelical people always do, that his own way was God's also. It happened, however, for the good of Germany, that this king's own way, to a great extent, *was* God's also,—(we will look at Carlyle's statement of that fact another day,)—and accordingly he maintained, and the ghost of him,—with the help of his son, whom he had like to have shot as a disobedient and dissipated character,—maintains to this day in Germany, such sacred domestic life as that of which you have an account in the above letter. Which, in peace, is entirely happy, for its own part ; and, in war, irresistible.

'Entirely *blessed*,' I had written first, too carelessly ; I have had to scratch out the 'blessed' and put in 'happy.' For blessing is only for the meek and merciful, and a German cannot be either ; he does not understand even the meaning of the words. In that is the intense, irreconcilable difference between the French and German natures. A Frenchman is selfish only when he is vile and lustful ; but a German, selfish in the purest states of virtue and morality. A Frenchman is arrogant only in ignorance ; but no quantity of learning ever makes a German modest. " Sir," says Albert Durer of his own work, (and he is the modestest German I know,) " it cannot be better done." Luther serenely damns the entire gospel of St. James, because St. James happens to be not precisely of his own opinions.

Accordingly, when the Germans get command of Lombardy, they bombard Venice, steal her pictures, (which they can't understand a single touch of,) and entirely ruin the country, morally and physically, leaving behind them misery, vice, and intense hatred of themselves, wherever their accursed feet have trodden. They do precisely the same thing by France,—crush her, rob her, leave her in misery of rage and shame ; and return home, smacking their lips, and singing Te Deums.

But when the French conquer England, their action upon it is entirely beneficent. Gradually, the country, from a nest of restless savages, becomes strong and glorious , and having good material to work upon, they make of us at last a nation stronger than themselves.

Then the strength of France perishes, virtually, through the folly of St. Louis ;—her piety evaporates, her lust gathers infectious power, and the modern Cité rises round the Sainte Chapelle.

It is a woful history. But St. Louis does not perish selfishly ; and perhaps is not wholly dead yet,—whatever Garibaldi and his red-jackets may think about him, and their ' Holy Republic.'

Meantime, Germany, through Geneva, works quaintly against France, in our British destiny, and makes an end of many a Sainte Chapelle, in our own sweet river islands. Read Froude's sketch of the Influence of the Reformation on Scottish Character, in his "Short studies on great subjects." And that would be enough for you to think of, this month; but as this letter is all made up of scraps, it may be as well to finish with this little private note on Luther's people, made last week.

4th March, 1874.—I have been horribly plagued and misguided by evangelical people, all my life; and most of all lately; but my mother was one, and my Scotch aunt; and I have yet so much of the super- stition left in me, that I can't help sometimes doing as evangelical people wish,—for all I know it comes to nothing.

One of them, for whom I still have some old liking left, sent me one of their horrible sausage-books the other day, made of chopped-up Bible; but with such a solemn and really pathetic adjuration to read a 'text' every morning, that, merely for old acquaintance' sake, I couldn't refuse. It is all one to me, now, whether I read my Bible, or my Homer, at one leaf or another; only I take the liberty, pace my evangelical friend, of looking up the contexts if I happen not to know them.

Now I was very much beaten and overtired yesterday, chiefly owing to a week of black fog, spent in looking

over a work of days and people long since dead,
and my 'text' this morning was, "Deal courageously,
and the Lord do that which seemeth Him good." It
sounds a very saintly, submissive, and useful piece of
advice; but I was not quite sure who gave it; and it
was evidently desirable to ascertain that.

For, indeed, it chances to be given, not by a saint
at all, but by quite one of the most self-willed people
on record in any history,—about the last in the world
to let the Lord do that which seemed Him good, if he
could help it, unless it seemed just as good to himself
also,—Joab the son of Zeruiah. The son, to wit, of
David's elder sister ; who, finding that it seemed good to
the Lord to advance the son of David's younger sister
to a place of equal power with himself, unhesitatingly
smites his thriving young cousin under the fifth rib,
while pretending to kiss him, and leaves him wallow-
ing in blood in the midst of the highway. But we
have no record of the pious or resigned expressions
he made use of on that occasion. We have no record,
either, of several other matters one would have liked
to know about these people. How it is, for instance,
that David has to make a brother of Saul's son ;—
getting, as it seems, no brotherly kindness—nor, more
wonderful yet, sisterly kindness—at his own fireside.
It is like a German story of the seventh son—or the
seventh bullet—as far as the brothers are concerned ;
but these sisters, had they also no love for their brave

young shepherd brother? Did they receive no coun-
tenance from him when he was king? Even for Zeruiah's sake, might he not on his death-bed have at least
allowed the Lord to do what seemed Him good with
Zeruiah's son, who had so well served him in his battles, (and so quietly in the matter of Bathsheba,) instead
of charging the wisdom of Solomon to find some
subtle way of preventing his hoar head from going
down to the grave in peace? My evangelical friend
will of course desire me not to wish to be wise above
that which is written. I am not to ask even who Zeruiah's husband was?—nor whether, in the West-end sense,
he was her husband at all?—Well; but if I only want
to be wise up to the meaning of what is written? I
find, indeed, nothing whatever said of David's elder
sister's lover;—but, of his younger sister's lover, I find
it written in this evangelical Book-Idol, in one place, that
his name was Ithra, an Israelite, and in another that
it was Jether, the Ishmaelite. Ithra or Jether, is no
matter; Israelite or Ishmaelite, perhaps matters not
much; but it matters a great deal that you should
know that this is an ill written, and worse trans-written,
human history, and not by any means 'Word of God;'
and that whatever issues of life, divine or human, there
may be in it, for you, can only be got by searching it; and
not by chopping it up into small bits and swallowing it
like pills. What a trouble there is, for instance, just now,
in all manner of people's minds, about Sunday keeping,

just because these evangelical people *will* swallow their bits of texts in an entirely indigestible state, without chewing them. Read your Bibles honestly and utterly, my scrupulous friends, and stand by the consequences,— if you have what true men call 'faith' In the first place, determine clearly, if there is a clear place in your brains to do it, whether you mean to observe the Sabbath as a Jew, or the day of the Resurrection, as a Christian. Do either thoroughly , you can't do both If you choose to keep the ' Sabbath,' in defiance of your great prophet, St. Paul, keep the new moons too, and the other fasts and feasts of the Jewish law , but even so, remember that the Son of Man is Lord of the Sabbath also, and that not only it is lawful to do good upon it, but unlawful, in the strength of what you call keeping one day Holy, to do Evil on other six days, and make those unholy ; and, finally, that neither new-moon keeping, nor Sabbath keeping, nor fasting, nor praying, will in anywise help an evangelical city like Edinburgh to stand in the judgment higher than Gomorrah, while her week-day arrangements for rent from her lower orders are as follows .—*

" We entered the first room by descending two steps It seemed to be an old coal-cellar, with an earthen floor, shining in many places from damp, and from a greenish

* Notes on Old Edinburgh · Edmonston and Douglas, 1869. Things may possibly have mended in some respects in the last five years, but they have assuredly, in the country villages, got tenfold worse

ooze which drained through the wall from a noxious collection of garbage outside, upon which a small window could have looked had it not been filled up with brown paper and rags. There was no grate, but a small fire smouldered on the floor, surrounded by heaps of ashes. The roof was unceiled, the walls were rough and broken, the only light came in from the open door, which let in unwholesome smells and sounds. No cow or horse could thrive in such a hole. It was abominable. It measured eleven feet by six feet, and the rent was 10*d.* per week, paid in advance. It was nearly dark at noon, even with the door open ; but as my eyes became accustomed to the dimness, I saw that the plenishings consisted of an old bed, a barrel with a flagstone on the top of it for a table, a three-legged stool, and an iron pot. A very ragged girl, sorely afflicted with ophthalmia, stood among the ashes doing nothing. She had never been inside a school or church. She did not know how to do anything, but 'did for her father and brother.' On a heap of straw, partly covered with sacking, which was the bed in which father, son, and daughter slept, the brother, ill with rheumatism and sore legs, was lying moaning from under a heap of filthy rags. He had been a baker 'over in the New Town,' but seemed not very likely to recover. It looked as if the sick man had crept into his dark, damp lair, just to die of hopelessness. The father was past work, but 'sometimes got an odd job to do.' The sick man had supported the three. It was hard to be godly, impossible to be cleanly, impossible to be healthy in such circumstances.

"The next room was entered by a low, dark, impeded passage about twelve feet long, too filthy to be traversed without a light. At the extremity of this was a dark winding stair which led up to four superincumbent storeys of crowded subdivided rooms ; and beyond this, to the right, a pitch-dark passage with a 'room' on either side It was not possible to believe that the most grinding greed could extort money from human beings for the tenancy of such dens as those to which this passage led. They were lairs into which a starving dog might creep to die, but nothing more. Opening a dilapidated door, we found ourselves in a recess nearly six feet high, and nine feet in length by five in breadth It was not absolutely dark, yet matches aided our investigations even at noonday. There was an earthen floor full of holes, in some of which water had collected. The walls were black and rotten, and alive with woodlice. There was no grate. The rent paid for this evil den, which was only ventilated by the chimney, is 1*s.* per week, or £2 12*s.* annually ! The occupier was a mason's labourer, with a wife and three children. He had come to Edinburgh in search of work, and could not afford a 'higher rent.' The wife said that her husband took the 'wee drap.' So would the President of the Temperance League himself if he were hidden away in such a hole. The contents of this lair on our first visit were a great heap of ashes and other refuse in one corner, some damp musty straw in another, a broken box in the third, with a battered tin pannikin upon it, and nothing else of any kind, saving two small children, nearly nude, covered with running sores, and pitiable from some eye disease. Their hair was not long, but felted into wisps, and alive with vermin. When we went in they were sitting among the ashes of an extinct fire, and blinked at the light from our matches. Here a neighbour said they sat all day, unless their mother was merciful enough to turn them into the gutter. We were there at eleven the following night, and found the mother, a decent, tidy body, at ' *hame.*' There was a small fire then, but no other light. She complained of little besides the darkness of the house, and said, in a tone of dull discontent, she supposed it was 'as good as such as they could expect in Edinburgh.' "

NOTES AND CORRESPONDENCE.

———◆———

To my great satisfaction, I am asked by a pleasant correspondent, where and what the picture of the Princess's Dream is. High up, in an out-of-the-way corner of the Academy of Venice, seen by no man—nor woman neither,—of all pictures in Europe the one I should choose for a gift, if a fairy queen gave me choice,—Victor Carpaccio's "Vision of St. Ursula."

The following letter, from the 'Standard,' is worth preserving.—

Sir,—For some time past the destruction of tons of young fry—viz., salmon, turbot, trout, soles, cod, whiting, etc.,—in fact, every fish that is to be found in the Thames,—has been enormous. I beg leave to say that it is now worse than ever, inasmuch as larger nets, and an increased number of them, are used, and the trade has commenced a month earlier than usual, from the peculiarity of the season.

At this time there are, at one part of the river, four or five vessels at work, which in one tide catch three tons of fry; this is sifted and picked over by hand, and about three per cent. of fry is all that can be picked out small enough for the London market. The remainder of course dies during the process, and is thrown overboard! Does the London consumer realize the fact that at least thirty tons a week of young fry are thus sacrificed? Do Londoners know that under the name of "whitebait" they eat a mixture largely composed of sprat fry, a fish which at Christmas cost 9d. a bushel, but which now fetches 2s. a quart, which is £3 4s a bushel? (Price regulated by Demand and Supply, you observe!—J. R.) It is bad enough that so many young salmon and trout are trapped and utterly wasted in these nets; but is it fair towards the public thus to diminish their supply of useful and cheap food?

Mr. Frank Buckland would faint, were he to see the wholesale destruction of young fry off Southend (on one fishing-ground only). I may truly say that the fishermen themselves are ashamed of the havoc they are making—well they may be; but who is to blame?

I have the honour to be, etc.,

Feb. 23.   PISCICULUS.

The following note, written long before the last Fors on fish, bears on some of the same matters, and may as well find place now. Of the Bishop to whom it alludes, I have also something to say in next, or next, Fors. The note itself refers to what I said about the defence of Pope, who, like all other gracious men, had grave faults; and who, like all other wise men, is intensely obnoxious to evangelical divines. I don't know what school of divines Mr. Elwyn belongs to, nor did I know his name when I wrote the note: I have been surprised, since, to see how good his work is; he writes with the precise pomposity of Macaulay, and in those worst and fatallest forms of fallacy which are true as far as they reach

"There is an unhappy wretch of a clergyman I read of in the papers—spending his life industriously in showing the meanness of Alexander Pope—and how Alexander Pope cringed, and lied. He cringed—yes—to his friends;—nor is any man good for much who will not play spaniel to his friend, or his mistress, on occasion;—to how many more than their friends do average clergymen cringe? I have had a Bishop go round the Royal Academy even with *me*,—pretending he liked painting, when he was eternally incapable of knowing anything whatever about it Pope lied also—alas, yes, for his vanity's sake. Very woful But he did not pass the whole of his life in trying to anticipate, or appropriate, or efface, other people's discoveries, as your modern men of science do so often; and for lying—any average partisan of religious dogma tells more lies in his pulpit in defence of what in his heart he knows to be indefensible, on any given Sunday, than Pope did in his whole life. Nay, how often is your clergyman himself nothing but a lie rampant—in the true old sense of the word,—creeping up into his pulpit pretending that he is there as a messenger of God, when he really took the place that he might be able to marry a pretty girl, and live like a 'gentleman' as he thinks. Alas! how infinitely more of a gentleman if he would but hold his foolish tongue, and get a living honestly—by street-sweeping, or any other useful occupation—instead of sweeping the dust of his own thoughts into people's eyes—as this 'biographer.' "

I shall have a good deal to say about human madness, in the course of Fors, the following letter, concerning the much less mischievous rabies of Dogs, is, however, also valuable. Note especially its closing paragraph. I omit a sentence here and there which seems to me unnecessary.

"On the 7th June last there appeared in the 'Macclesfield Guardian' newspaper a letter on Rabies and the muzzling and confining of Dogs, signed 'Beth-Gêlert.' That communication contained several facts and opinions relating to the disease the possible causes of the same; and the uselessness and cruelty of muzzling and confinement as a preventive to it The first-named unnatural practice has been condemned (as was there shown) by no less authority than the leading medical journal of England,—which has termed muzzling '*a great practical mistake, and one which cannot fail to have an injurious effect both upon the health and temper of dogs ; for, although rabies is a dreadful thing, dogs ought not, any more than men, to be constantly treated as creatures likely to go mad.*'

" This information and judgment, however, seem insufficient to convince some minds, even although they have no observations or arguments to urge in opposition.　It may be useful to the public to bring forward an opinion on the merits of that letter expressed by the late Thomas Turner, of Manchester, who was not only a member of the Council, but one of the ablest and most experienced surgeons in Europe.　The words of so eminent a professional man cannot but be considered valuable, and must have weight with the sensible and sincere ; though on men of an opposite character all evidence, all reason, is too often utterly cast away.

"MOSLEY STREET, *June* 8, 1873

" ' Dear ——,—Thanks for your sensible letter.　It contains great and *kind* truths, and such as humanity should applaud. On the subject you write about there is a large amount of ignorance both in and out of the profession.

" Ever yours,

" THOMAS TURNER."

" In addition to the foregoing statement of the founder of the Manchester Royal School of Medicine and Surgery, the opinion shall now be given of one of the best veterinarians in London, who, writing on the above letter in the ' Macclesfield Guardian,' observed,—' *With regard to your paper on muzzling dogs, I feel certain from observation that the restraint put upon them by the muzzle is productive of evil, and has a tendency to cause fits, etc.*

" Rabies, originally spontaneous, was probably created, like many other evils which afflict humanity, by the viciousness, ignorance, and selfishness of man himself. *'Man's inhumanity to man makes countless thousands mourn,'*—wrote the great peasant and national poet of Scotland. He would have uttered even a wider and more embracing truth had he said, man's inhumanity to his *fellow-creatures* makes countless millions mourn. Rabies is most prevalent amongst the breeds of dogs bred and maintained for the atrocious sports of 'the pit,' they are likewise the most dangerous when victims to that dreadful malady. Moreover, dogs kept to worry other animals are also among those most liable to the disease, and the most to be feared when mad. But, on the other hand, dogs who live as the friends and companions of men of true humanity, and never exposed to annoyance or ill-treatment, remain gentle and affectionate even under the excruciating agonies of this dire disease. Delabere Blaine, first an army surgeon and sub- sequently the greatest veterinarian of this or probably of any other nation, tells us in his 'Canine Pathology,'—

" 'It will sensibly affect any one to witness the earnest, imploring look I have often seen from the unhappy sufferers under this dreadful malady. The strongest attachment has been manifested to those around during their utmost sufferings, and the parched tongue has been carried over the hands and feet of those who noticed them, with more than usual fondness. This disposition has continued to the last moment of life,—in many cases, with- out one manifestation of any inclination to bite, or to do the smallest harm.'

" Here is another instance of ' with whatsoever measure ye mete, it shall be measured to you again.' The cruelty of man, as it ever does, recoils, like a viper, ultimately on man. He who invests in the Bank of Vice receives back his capital with compound interest at a high rate and to the uttermost farthing

"When a mad dog bites many people, he sometimes quits scores for a long, long arrear of brutalities, insults, and oppression inflicted upon him by the baser portion of mankind :—the hard blow, the savage kick, the loud curse, the vile annoyance, the insulting word, the starving meal, the carrion food, the shortened chain, the rotten straw, the dirty kennel (appropriate name), the bitter winter's night, the parching heat of summer, the dull and dreary years of hopeless imprisonment, the thousand aches which patient merit of the unworthy takes, are represented, culminate there , and the cup man has poisoned, man is forced to drink.

"All these miseries are often, too often, the lot of this most affectionate creature, who has truly been called 'our faithful friend, gallant protector, and useful servant.'

"No muzzling, murder, or incarceration tyrannically inflicted on this much-enduring, much-insulted slave by his master, will ever extirpate rabies. No abuse of the wondrous creature beneficently bestowed by the Omniscient and Almighty on ungrateful man, to be the friend of the poor and the guardian of the rich, will ever extirpate rabies. Mercy and justice would help us much more

"In many lands the disease is utterly unknown,—in the land of Egypt, for example, where dogs swarm in all the towns and villages. Yet the follower of Mohammed, more humane than the follower of Christ,—to our shame be it spoken,—neither imprisons, muzzles, nor murders them. England, it is believed, never passed such an Act of Parliament as this before the present century There is, certainly, in the laws of Canute a punishment awarded to the man whose dog went mad, and by his negligence wandered up and down the country. A far more sensible measure than our own. Canute punished the *man*, not the *dog*. Also, in Edward the Third's reign, all owners of fighting dogs whose dogs were found wandering about the streets of London were fined. Very different species of legislation from the brainless or brutal Dog's Act of 1871, passed by a number of men, not one of whom it is probable either knew or cared to know anything of the nature of the creature they legislated about, not even that he perspires, not by means of his skin, but performs this vital function by means of his tongue, and that to muzzle *him* is tantamount to coating the skin of a man all over with paint or gutta-percha. Such selfishness and cruelty in this age appears to give evidence towards proof of the assertion made by our greatest writer on Art,—that 'we are now getting cruel in our avarice,'—'our hearts, of iron and clay, have hurled the Bible in the face of our God, and fallen down to grovel before Mammon.'—If not, how is it that we can so abuse one of the Supreme's most choicest works, —a creature sent to be man's friend, and whose devotion so often 'puts to shame all human attachments'?

"We are reaping what we have sown Rabies certainly seems on the increase in this district,—in whose neighbourhood, it is stated, muzzling was first practised It may spread more widely if we force a crop. The best way to check it, is to do our duty to the noble creature the Almighty has entrusted to us, and treat him with the humanity and affection he so eminently deserves. To deprive him of liberty and exercise; to chain him like a felon; to debar him from access to his natural medicine, to prevent him from following the overpowering instincts of his being and the laws of Nature, is conduct revolting to reason and religion.

"The disease of rabies comes on by degrees, not suddenly. Its symptoms can easily be read Were knowledge more diffused, people would know the approach of the malady, and take timely precautions To do as we now do,—namely, drive the unhappy creatures insane, into an agonizing sickness by sheer ignorance or inhumanity, and then, because one is ill, tie up the mouths of the healthy, and unnaturally restrain all the rest, is it not the conduct of idiots rather than of reasonable beings?

"Why all this hubbub about a disease which causes less loss of life than almost any other complaint known, and whose fatal effects can, in almost every case, be surely and certainly prevented by a surgeon? If our lawgivers and lawmakers (who, by the way, although the House of Commons is crowded with lawyers, do not in these times draw Acts of Parliament so that they can be comprehended, without the heavy cost of going to a superior court,) wish to save human life, let them educate the hearts as well as heads of Englishmen, and give more attention to boiler and colliery explosions, railway smashes, and rotten ships; to the overcrowding and misery of the poor; to the adulteration of food and medicines. Also, to dirt, municipal stupidity, and neglect; by which one city alone, Manchester, loses annually above three thousand lives.

"I am, your humble servant,

"BETH-GÊLERT."

FORS CLAVIGERA.

LETTER THE 41st.

BERNARD THE HAPPY.

PARIS, *1st April*, 1874.

I FIND there are still primroses in Kent, and that it is possible still to see blue sky in London in the early morning. It was entirely pure as I drove down past my old Denmark Hill gate, bound for Cannon Street Station, on Monday morning last ; gate, closed now on me for evermore, that used to open gladly enough when I came back to it from work in Italy. Now, father and mother and nurse all dead, and the roses of the spring, prime or late—what are they to me ?

But I want to know, rather, what are they to *you ?* What have *you*, workers in England, to do with April, or May, or June either ; your mill-wheels go no faster for the sunshine, do they ? and you can't get more smoke up the chimneys because more sap goes up the trunks. Do you so much as know or care who May was, or her son, Shepherd of the heathen souls, so despised of you

Christians? Nevertheless, I have a word or two to say
to you in the light of the hawthorn blossom, only you
must read some rougher ones first. I have printed the
June Fors together with this, because I want you to read
the June one first, only the substance of it is not good
for the May-time; but read it, and when you get to near
the end, where it speaks of the distinctions between the
sins of the hot heart and the cold, come back to this,
for I want you to think in the flush of May what strength
is in the flush of the heart also. You will find that in
all my late books (during the last ten years) I have
summed the needful virtue of men under the terms of
gentleness and justice; gentleness being the virtue which
distinguishes gentlemen from churls, and justice that
which distinguishes honest men from rogues. Now gentleness may be defined as the Habit or State of Love;
the Red Carita of Giotto (see account of her in Letter
Seventh); and ungentleness or clownishness, the opposite State or Habit of Lust.

Now there are three great loves that rule the souls of
men : the love of what is lovely in creatures, and of what
is lovely in things, and what is lovely in report. And
these three loves have each their relative corruption, a
lust—the lust of the flesh, the lust of the eyes, and the
pride of life

And, as I have just said, a gentleman is distinguished
from a churl by the purity of sentiment he can reach in
all these three passions : by his imaginative love, as

opposed to lust , his imaginative possession of wealth as opposed to avarice ; his imaginative desire of honour as opposed to pride.

And it is quite possible for the simplest workman or labourer for whom I write to understand what the feelings of a gentleman are, and share them, if he will ; but the crisis and horror of this present time are that its desire of money, and the fulness of luxury dishonestly attainable by common persons, are gradually making churls of all men ; and the nobler passions are not merely disbelieved, but even the conception of them seems ludicrous to the impotent churl mind ; so that, to take only so poor an instance of them as my own life—because I have passed it in almsgiving, not in fortune-hunting ; because I have laboured always for the honour of others, not my own, and have chosen rather to make men look to Turner and Luini, than to form or exhibit the skill of my own hand ; because I have lowered my rents, and assured the comfortable lives of my poor tenants, instead of taking from them all I could force for the roofs they needed ; because I love a wood walk better than a London street, and would rather watch a seagull fly than shoot it, and rather hear a thrush sing than eat it , finally, because I never disobeyed my mother, because I have honoured all women with solemn worship, and have been kind even to the unthankful and the evil ; therefore the hacks of English art and literature wag their heads at me, and the poor wretch who pawns the dirty linen of his soul daily for a bottle of sour wine and a cigar, talks of the "effeminate sentimentality of Ruskin."

Now of these despised sentiments, which in all ages have distinguished the gentleman from the churl, the first is that reverence for womanhood which, even through all the cruelties of the Middle Ages, developed itself with increasing power until the thirteenth century, and became consummated in the imagination of the Madonna, which ruled over all the highest arts and purest thoughts of that age.

To the common Protestant mind the dignities ascribed to the Madonna have been always a violent offence ; they are one of the parts of the Catholic faith which are openest to reasonable dispute, and least comprehensible by the average realistic and materialist temper of the Reformation. But after the most careful examination, neither as adversary nor as friend, of the influences of Catholicism for good and evil, I am persuaded that the worship of the Madonna has been one of its noblest and most vital graces, and has never been otherwise than productive of true holiness of life and purity of character. I do not enter into any question as to the truth or fallacy of the idea ; I no more wish to defend the historical or theological position of the Madonna than that of St. Michael or St. Christopher ; but I am certain that to the habit of reverent belief in, and contemplation of, the character ascribed to the heavenly hierarchies, we must ascribe the highest results yet achieved in human nature, and that it is neither Madonna-worship nor saint-worship, but the evangelical self-worship and hell-worship—gloating, with an imagination as unfounded as it is foul, over the torments of the damned, instead of the glories of the blest,—which have in reality degraded the languid powers of Christianity to their present state of shame and reproach. There has probably not been an innocent cottage home throughout the length and breadth of Europe during the whole period of vital Christianity, in which the imagined presence of the Madonna has not given sanctity to the humblest duties, and comfort to the sorest trials of the lives of women ; and every brightest and loftiest achievement of the arts and strength of manhood has been the fulfilment of the assured prophecy of the poor Israelite maiden, " He that is mighty hath magnified me, and Holy is His name." What we are about to substitute for such magnifying in our modern wisdom, let the reader judge from two slight things that chanced to be noticed by me in my walk round Paris I generally go first to Our Lady's Church, for though the towers and most part of the walls are now merely the modern model of the original building, much of the portal sculpture is still genuine, and especially the greater part of the lower arcades of the north-west door, where the common entrance is. I always held these such valuable pieces of the thirteenth century work that I had them cast, in mass, some years ago, brought away casts, eight feet high by twelve wide, and gave them to the

Architectural Museum. So as I was examining these, and laboriously gleaning what was left of the old work among M. Violet le Duc's fine fresh heads of animals and points of leaves, I saw a brass plate in the back of one of the niches, where the improperly magnified saints used to be At first I thought it was over one of the usual almsboxes which have a right to be at church entrances (if anywhere) ; but catching sight of an English word or two on it, I stopped to read, and read to the following effect .—

"F. du Larin,
office
of the
Victoria Pleasure Trips
And Excursions to Versailles.
Excursions to the Battle-fields round Paris.

" A four-horse coach with an English guide starts daily from Notre Dame Cathedral, at $10\frac{1}{2}$ a.m. for Versailles, by the Bois de Boulogne, St. Cloud, Montretout, and Ville d'Avray Back in Paris at $5\frac{1}{2}$ p m. Fares must be secured one day in advance at the entrance of Notre Dame.

The Manager, H. du Larin."

" Magnificat anima mea Dominum, quia respexit humilitatem ancillæ Suæ" Truly it seems to be time that God should again regard the lowliness of His hand-maiden, now that she has become keeper of the coach office for excursions to Versailles. The arrangement becomes still more perfect in the objects of this Christian joyful pilgrimage (*from* Canterbury, as it were, instead of to it), the " Battle-fields round Paris ! "

From Notre Dame I walked back into the livelier parts of the city, though in no very lively mood ; but recovered some tranquillity in the Marché aux fleurs, which is a pleasant spectacle in April, and then made some circuit of the Boulevards, where, as the third Fors would have it, I suddenly came in view of one of the temples of the modern superstition, which is to replace Mariolatry. For it seems that human creatures *must* imagine something or someone in Apotheosis, and the Assumption of the Virgin, and Titian's or Tintoret's views on that matter being held reasonable no more, apotheosis of some other power follows as a matter of course. Here accordingly is one of the modern hymns on the Advent of Spring, which replace now in France the sweet Cathedral services of the Mois de Marie. It was printed in vast letters on a white sheet, dependent at the side of the porch or main entrance to the fur shop of the " Compagnie Anglo-Russe."

" Le printemps s'annonce avec son gracieux cortège de rayons et de fleurs. Adieu, l'hiver ! C'en est bien fini ! Et cependant il faut que toutes ces fourrures soient enlevées, vendues, données, dans ces 6 jours. C'est une aubaine inesperée, un placement fabuleux ; car, qu'on ne l'oublie pas, la fourrure vraie, la belle, la riche, a toujours sa valeur intrinsique.   Et, comme couronnement de cette sorte d'APOTHÉOSE la Cᴵᵉ· Anglo-Russe remet gratis à tout acheteur un talisman merveilleux pour conserver la fourrure pendant 10 saisons"

"Unto Adam also, and to his wife, did the Lord God make coats of skins and clothed them."

The Anglo-Russian company having now superseded Divine labour in such matters, you have also, instead of the grand old Dragon-Devil with his "Ye shall be as Gods, knowing good and evil," only a little weasel of a devil with an ermine tip to his tail, advising you "Ye shall be as Gods, buying your skins cheap."

I am a simpleton, am I, to quote such an exploded book as Genesis?   My good wiseacre readers, I know as many flaws in the book of Genesis as the best of you, but I knew the book before I knew its flaws, while you know the flaws, and never have known the book, nor can know it.   And it is at present much the worse for you , for indeed the stories of this book of Genesis have been the nursery tales of men mightiest whom the world has yet seen in art, and policy, and virtue, and none of you will write better stories for your children, yet awhile. And your little Cains will learn quickly enough to ask if they are their brother's keepers, and your little Fathers of Canaan merrily enough to show their own father's nakedness without dread either of banishment or male-diction ; but many a day will pass, and their evil generations vanish with it, in that sudden nothingness of the wicked, " He passed away, and lo, he was not," before one will again rise, of whose death there may remain the Divine tradition, " He walked with God, and was not, for God took him." Apotheosis ! How the dim hope of it haunts even the last degradation of men ; and through the six thousand years from Enoch, and the vague Greek ages which dreamed of their twin-hero stars, declines, in this final stage of civilization, into dependence on the sweet promise of the Anglo-Russian tempter, with his ermine tail, " Ye shall be as Gods, and buy cat-skin cheap."

So it must be. I know it, my good wiseacres. You can have no more Queens of Heaven, nor assumptions of triumphing saints. Even your simple country Queen of May, whom once you worshipped for a goddess—has not little Mr. Faraday analysed her, and proved her to consist of charcoal and water, combined under what the Duke of Argyll calls the " reign of law " ? Your once fortune-guiding stars, which used to twinkle in a mysterious manner, and to make you wonder what they were,—everybody knows what they are now: only hydrogen gas, and they stink as they twinkle. My wiseacre acquaintances, it is very fine, doubtless, for you to know all these things, who have plenty of money in your pockets, and nothing particular to burden your chemical minds ; but for the poor, who have nothing in their pockets, and the wretched, who have much on their hearts, what in the world is the good of knowing that the only heaven they have to go to is a large gaso-meter?

" Poor and wretched ! " you answer. " But when once everybody is convinced that heaven is a large·gasometer, and when we have turned all the world into a small gasometer, and can drive round it by steam, and in forty minutes be back again where we were,—nobody will be poor or wretched any more. Sixty pounds on the square inch,—can anybody be wretched under that general application of high pressure ? "

(Assisi, 15th April.)

Good wiseacres, yes, it seems to me, at least, more than probable : but if not, and you all find yourselves rich and merry, with steam legs and steel hearts, I am well assured there will be found yet room, where your telescopes have not reached, nor can,—grind you their lenses ever so finely,—room for the quiet souls, who choose for their part, poverty, with light and peace.

I am writing at a narrow window, which looks out on some broken tiles and a dead wall. A wall dead in the profoundest sense, you wiseacres would think it. Six hundred years old, and as strong as when it was built, and paying nobody any interest, and still less commission, on the cost of repair. Both sides of the street, or path-way rather,—it is not nine feet wide,—are similarly built with solid blocks of grey marble, arched rudely above the windows, with here and there a cross on the key-stones.

If I chose to rise from my work and walk a hundred yards down this street (if one may so call the narrow path between grey walls, as quiet and lonely as a sheep-walk on Shap Fells,) I should come to a small prison-like door ; and over the door is a tablet of white marble let into the grey, and on the tablet is written, in con-tracted Latin, what in English signifies :—

> " Here, Bernard the Happy*
> Received St. Francis of Assisi,
> And saw him, in ecstasy."

Good wiseacres, you believe nothing of the sort, do you ? Nobody ever yet was in ecstasy, you think, till now, when they may buy cat-skin cheap ?

Do you believe in Blackfriars Bridge, then ; and admit that some day or other there must have been reason to call it " Black Friar's " ? As surely as the bridge stands over Thames, and St. Paul's above it, these two men, Paul and Francis, had their ecstasies, in bygone days, concerning other matters than ermine tails ; and still the same ecstasies, or effeminate sentiments, are possible to human creatures, believe it or not as you will. I am

---

* " Bernard the happy.' The Beato of Mont Oliveto ; not Bernard of Clairvaux The entire inscription is, " received St. Francis of Assisi to supper and bed " ; but if I had written it so, it would have appeared that St. Francis's ecstasy was in consequence of his getting his supper

not now, whatever the ' Pall Mall Gazette ' may think, an
ecstatic person myself. But thirty years ago I knew
once or twice what joy meant, and have not forgotten
the feeling ; nay, even so little a while as two years ago,
I had it back again—for a day. And I can assure you,
good wiseacres, there is such a thing to be had ; but
not in cheap shops, nor, I was going to say, for money ;
yet in a certain sense it is buyable—by forsaking all
that a man hath. Buyable—literally enough—the freehold Elysian field at that price, but not a doit cheaper ;
and I believe, at this moment, the reason my voice has
an uncertain sound, the reason that this design of mine
stays unhelped, and that only a little group of men and
women, moved chiefly by personal regard, stand with me
in a course so plain and true, is that I have not yet
given myself to it wholly, but have halted between good
and evil, and sit still at the receipt of custom, and am
always looking back from the plough.

It is not wholly my fault this. There seem to me
good reasons why I should go on with my work in
Oxford ; good reasons why I should have a house of
my own with pictures and library ; good reasons why
I should still take interest from the bank ; good reasons
why I should make myself as comfortable as I can,
wherever I go ; travel with two servants, and have a
dish of game at dinner. It is true, indeed, that I have
given the half of my goods and more to the poor ; it
is true also that the work in Oxford is not a matter

of pride, but of duty with me; it is true that I think it wiser to live what seems to other people a rational and pleasant, not an enthusiastic, life; and that I serve my servants at least as much as they serve me. But, all this being so, I find there is yet something wrong; I have no peace, still less ecstasy. It seems to me as if one had indeed to wear camel's hair instead of dress coats before one can get that; and I was looking at St. Francis's camel's-hair coat yesterday (they have it still in the sacristy), and I don't like the look of it at all; the Anglo-Russian Company's wear is ever so much nicer,—let the devil at least have this due.

And he must have a little more due even than this. It is not at all clear to me how far the Beggar and Pauper Saint, whose marriage with the Lady Poverty I have come here to paint from Giotto's dream of it,— how far, I say, the mighty work he did in the world was owing to his vow of poverty, or diminished by it. If he had been content to preach love alone, whether among poor or rich, and if he had understood that love, for all God's creatures, was one and the same blessing; and that, if he was right to take the doves out of the fowler's hand, that they might build their nests, he was himself wrong when he went out in the winter's night on the hills, and made for himself dolls of snow, and said, "Francis, these—behold—these are thy wife and thy children." If instead of quitting his father's trade, that he might nurse lepers, he had made his father's trade holy and pure, and honourable more than beggary, perhaps at this day the Black Friars might yet have had an unruined house by Thames shore, and the children of his native village not be standing in the porches of the temple built over his tomb, to ask alms of the infidel.

FORS CLAVIGERA.

LETTER THE 42nd.

MISERICORDIA

I MUST construct my letters still, for a while, of swept-up fragments; every day provokes me to write new matter; but I must not lose the fruit of the old days. Here is some worth picking up, though ill-ripened for want of sunshine, (the little we had spending itself on the rain,) last year.

1st August, 1873.

" Not being able to work steadily this morning, because there was a rainbow half a mile broad, and violet-bright, on the shoulders of the Old Man of Coniston—(by calling it half a mile broad, I mean that half a mile's breadth of mountain was covered by it,—and by calling it violet-bright, I mean that the violet zone of it came pure against the grey rocks; and note, by the way, that essentially all the colours of the rainbow are secondary ;—yellow exists only as a line—red as a line—blue as a line ; but the zone itself is of varied orange, green, and violet,)—not being able, I say, for steady work, I opened an old diary of 1849, and as the third Fors would have it, at this extract from the Letters of Lady Mary Wortley Montagu.

(Venice.)

" The Prince of Saxony went to see the Arsenal three days ago, waited on by a numerous nobility of both sexes ; the Bucentaur was adorned and launched, a magnificent collation given ; and we sailed a little in it. I was in company with the Signora Justiniani Gradenigo and Signora Marina Crizzo. There were two cannons founded in his (the Prince of Saxony's) presence, and a galley built and launched in an hour's time." (Well may Dante speak of that busy Arsenal !)

" Last night there was a concert of voices and instruments at the Hospital of the Incurabili, where there were two guls that in the opinion of all people excel either Faustina or Cuzzoni.

" I am invited to-morrow to the Foscarini to dinner, which is to be followed by a concert and a ball."

The account of a regatta follows, in which the various nobles had boats costing £1000 sterling each, none less than £500, and enough of them to look like a little fleet. The Signora Pisani Mocenigo's represented the Chariot of the Night, drawn by four sea-horses, and showing the rising of the moon, accompanied with stars, the statues on each side representing the Hours, to the number of twenty-four.

Pleasant times, these, for Venice ! one's Bucentaur

launched, wherein to eat, buoyantly, a magnificent collation—beautiful ladies driving their ocean steeds in the
Chariot of the Night—beautiful songs, at the Hospital
of the Incurabili. Much bettered, these, from the rough
days when one had to row and fight for life, thought
Venice; better days still, in the nineteenth century,
being—as she appears to believe now—in store for her.

You thought, I suppose, that in writing those numbers of Fors last year from Venice and Verona, I was
idling, or digressing?

Nothing of the kind. The business of Fors is to tell
you of Venice and Verona; and many things of them.

You don't care about Venice and Verona? Of course
not. Who does? And I beg you to observe that
the day is coming when, exactly in the same sense,
active working men will say to any antiquarian who
purposes to tell them something of England, "We
don't care about England." And the antiquarian will
answer, just as I have answered you now, "Of course
not. Who does?"

Nay, the saying has been already said to me, and
by a wise and good man. When I asked, at the end
of my inaugural lecture at Oxford, "Will you, youths of
England, make your country again a royal throne of
kings, a sceptred isle, for all the world a source of
light—a centre of peace?"—my University friends came
to me, with grave faces, to remonstrate against irrelevant
and Utopian topics of that nature being introduced in

lectures on art; and a very dear American friend wrote to me, when I sent the lecture to him, in some such terms as these: "Why will you diminish your real influence for good, by speaking as if England could now take any dominant place in the world? How many millions, think you, are there here, of the activest spirits of their time, who care nothing for England, and would read no farther, after coming upon such a passage?"

That England deserves little care from any man nowadays, is fatally true; that in a century more she will be—where Venice is—among the dead of nations, is far more than probable. And yet—that you do not care for dead Venice, is the sign of your own ruin; and that the Americans do not care for dying England, is only the sign of their inferiority to her.

For this dead Venice once taught us to be merchants, sailors, and gentlemen; and this dying England taught the Americans all they have of speech, or thought, hitherto. What thoughts they have not learned from England are foolish thoughts; what words they have not learned from England, unseemly words; the vile among them not being able even to be humorous parrots, but only obscene mocking birds. An American republican woman, lately, describes a child which "like cherubim and seraphim continually did cry,"* such their feminine learning of the European fashions of 'Te Deum'! And, as I tell

* 'Pall Mall Gazette,' July 31st, 1873

you, Venice in like manner taught us, when she and we were honest, our marketing, and our manners. Then she began trading in pleasure, and souls of men, before us ; followed that Babylonish trade to her death,—we nothing loth to imitate, so plausible she was, in her mythic gondola, and Chariot of the Night ! But where her pilotage has for the present carried her, and is like to carry *us*, it may be well to consider. And therefore I will ask you to glance back to my twentieth letter, giving account of the steam music, the modern Tasso's echoes, practised on her principal lagoon. That is her present manner, you observe, of "whistling *at her darg*." But for festivity *after* work, or altogether superseding work—launching one's adorned Bucentaur for collation—let us hear what she is doing in that kind.

From the Rinnovamento (Renewal, or Revival,) "Gazette of the people of Venice" of 2nd July, 1872, I print, in my terminal notes, a portion of one of their daily correspondent's letters, describing his pleasures of the previous day, of which I here translate a few pregnant sentences.

"I embarked on a little steamboat. It was elegant— it was vast. But its contents were enormously greater than its capacity. The little steamboat overflowed* with men, women, and boys. The Commandant, a proud young man, cried, 'Come in, come in !' and the

* "Rigurgitava" gushed or gorged up , as a bottle which you have filled too full and too fast.

crowd became always more close, and one could scarcely breathe" (the heroic exhortations of the proud youth leading his public to this painful result). "All at once a delicate person * of the piazza, feeling herself unwell, cried 'I suffocate.' The Commandant perceived that suffocation did veritably prevail, and gave the word of command, 'Enough.'

"In eighteen minutes I had the good fortune to land safe at the establishment, 'The Favourite.' And here my eyes opened for wonder. In truth, only a respectable force of will could have succeeded in transforming this place, only a few months ago still desert and uncultivated, into a site of delights Long alleys, grassy carpets, small mountains, charming little banks, châlets, solitary and mysterious paths, and then an interminable covered way which conducts to the bathing establishment ; and in that, attendants dressed in mariners' dresses, a most commodious basin, the finest linen, and the most regular and solicitous service

"Surprised, and satisfied, I plunged myself cheerfully into the sea. After the bath, is prescribed a walk. Obedient to the dictates of hygiene, I take my returning way along the pleasant shore of the sea to 'The Favourite.' A châlet, or rather an immense salon, is become a con-

---

* Sensale, an interesting Venetian word The fair on the Feast of the Ascension at Venice became in mellifluous brevity, 'Sensa,' and the most ornamental of the ware purchasable at it, therefore, Sensale

A ' Holy-Thursday-Fairing," feeling herself unwell, would be the properest translation.

cert room. And, in fact, an excellent orchestra is executing therein most chosen pieces. The artists are all endued in dress coats, and wear white cravats. I hear with delight a pot-pourri from Faust. I then take a turn through the most vast park, and visit the Restaurant.

"To conclude. The Lido has no more need to become a place of delights. It is, in truth, already become so.

"All honour to the brave who have effected the marvellous transformation."

Onori ai bravi !—Honour to the brave ! Yes ; in all times, among all nations, that is entirely desirable. You know I told you, in last Fors, that to honour the brave dead was to be our second child's lesson. None the less expedient if the brave we have to honour be alive, instead of long dead. Here are our modern Venetian troubadours, in white cravats, celebrating the victories of their Hardicanutes with collection of choicest melody—pot-pourri—hotch-potch, from Faust. And, indeed, is not this a notable conquest which resuscitated Venice has made of her Lido ? Where all was vague sea-shore, now, behold, "little mountains, mysterious paths." Those unmanufactured mountains—Eugeneans and Alps—seen against the sunset, are not enough for the vast mind of Venice born again, nor the canals between her palaces mysterious enough paths. Here are mountains to our perfect mind, and more solemn ways,—a new kingdom for us, conquered by the brave.   Conquest, you observe also, just of the kind which in our 'Times' newspaper is honoured always in like manner, 'Private Enterprise.'   The only question is, whether the privacy of your enterprise is always as fearless of exposure as it used to be,—or even, the enterprise of it as enterprising.   Let me tell you a little of the private enterprise of dead Venice, that you may compare it with that of the living.

You doubted me just now, probably, when I told you that Venice taught you to be sailors   You thought your Drakes and Grenvilles needed no such masters No ! but a hundred years before Sir Francis's time, the blind captain of a Venetian galley,—of one of those things which the Lady Mary saw built in an hour,— won the empire of the East.   You did fine things in the Baltic, and before Sebastopol, with your ironclads and your Woolwich infants, did you ?   Here was a piece of fighting done from the deck of a rowed boat, which came to more good, it seems to me.

"The Duke of Venice had disposed his fleet in one line along the sea-wall (of Constantinople), and had cleared the battlements with his shot (of stones and arrows) ; but still the galleys dared not take ground. But the Duke of Venice, though he was old (ninety) and stone-blind, stood, all armed, at the head of his galley, and had the gonfalon of St. Mark before him ; and he called to his people to ground his ship, or they should die for it. So they ran the ship aground, and leaped out, and carried St. Mark's gonfalon to the shore before the Duke. Then the Venetians, seeing their Duke's galley ashore, followed him; and they planted the flag of St Mark on the walls, and took twenty-five towers."

The good issue of which piece of pantaloon's play was that the city itself, a little while after, with due help from the French, was taken, and that the crusading army proceeded thereon to elect a new Emperor of the Eastern Empire.

Which office six French Barons, and six Venetian, being appointed to bestow, and one of the French naming first the Duke of Venice, he had certainly been declared Emperor, but one of the Venetians themselves, Pantaleone Barbo, declaring that no man could be Duke of Venice, and Emperor too, gave his word for Baldwin of Flanders, to whom accordingly the throne was given; while to the Venetian State was offered, with the consent of all, if they chose to hold it—about a third of the whole Roman Empire!

Venice thereupon deliberates with herself. Her own present national territory—the true 'State' of Venice— is a marsh, which you can see from end to end of;— some wooden houses, half afloat, and others wholly afloat, in the canals of it; and a total population, in round numbers, about as large as that of our parish of Lambeth. Venice feels some doubt whether, out of this wild duck's nest, and with that number of men, she can at once safely, and in all the world's sight, undertake to govern Lacedæmon, Ægina, Ægos Potamos, Crete, and half the Greek islands; nevertheless, she thinks she will try a little 'private enterprise' upon them. So in 1207 the Venetian Senate published an edict by which there was granted to all Venetian citizens permission to arm, at their own expense, war-galleys, and to subdue, if they could manage it in that private manner, such islands and Greek towns of the Archipelago as might seem to them what we call "eligible residences," the Senate graciously giving them leave to keep whatever they could get. Whereupon certain Venetian merchants —proud young men—stood, as we see them standing now on their decks on the Riva, crying to the crowd, 'Montate! Montate!' and without any help from steam, or encumbrance from the markets of Ascension Day, rowed and sailed—somewhat *outside* the Lido. Mark Dandolo took Gallipoli; Mark Sanudo, Naxos, Paros, and Melos;—(you have heard of marbles and Venuses coming from those places, have not you?)—Marin Dandolo, Andros; Andrea Ghisi, Micone and Scyros; Dominico Michieli, Ceos; and Philocola Navigieri, the island of Vulcan himself, Lemnos. Took them, and kept them also! (not a little to our present sorrow; for, being good Christians, these Venetian gentlemen made wild work among the Parian and Melian gods) It was not till 1570 that the twenty-first Venetian Duke of Melos was driven out by the Turks, and the career of modern white-cravated Venice virtually begun.

"Honour to the brave!" Yes, in God's name, and by all manner of means! And dishonour to the cowards: but, my good Italian and good English acquaintances, are you so sure, then, you know which is which? Nay, are you honestly willing to acknowledge there is any difference? Heaven be praised if you are!—but I thought your modern gospel was, that all were alike? Here's the 'Punch' of last week lying beside me, for instance, with its normal piece of pathos upon the advertisements of death. Dual deaths this time; and pathetic epitaphs on the Bishop of Winchester and the Baron Bethell. The best it can honestly say, (and 'Punch,' as far as I know papers, is an honest one,) is that the Bishop was a pleasant kind of person; and the best it can say for the Chancellor is, that he was witty;—but, fearing that something more might be expected, it smooths all down with a sop of popular varnish, "How good the worst of us!—how bad the best!" Alas, Mr. Punch, is it come to this? and is there to be no more knocking down, then? and is your last scene in future to be—shaking hands with the devil?—clerical pantaloon in white cravat asking a blessing on the reconciliation, and the drum and pipe finishing with a pot-pourri from Faust?

A popular tune, truly, everywhere, nowadays—"Devil's hotch-potch," and listened to "avec delices!" And, doubtless, pious Republicans on their death-beds will have a care to bequeath it, rightly played, to their children, before they go to hear it, divinely executed, in their own blessed country.

"How good the worst of us !—how bad the best!" Jeanie Deans, and St. Agnes, and the Holy Thursday fairing, all the same!

My good working readers, I will try to-day to put you more clearly in understanding of this modern gospel,—of what truth there is in it—for some there is,—and of what pestilent evil.

I call it a modern gospel : in its deepest truth it is as old as Christianity. "This man receiveth sinners, and eateth with them." And it was the most distinctive character of Christianity. Here was a new, astonishing religion indeed, one had heard before of righteousness ; before of resurrection ;—never before of mercy to sin, or fellowship with it.

But it is only in strictly modern times (that is to say, within the last hundred years) that this has been fixed on, by a large sect of thick-headed persons, as the *essence* of Christianity,—nay, as so much its essence, that to be an extremely sinful sinner is deliberately announced by them as the best of qualifications for becoming an extremely Christian Christian.

But all the teachings of Heaven are given—by sad law—in so obscure, nay, often in so ironical manner, that a blockhead necessarily reads them wrong. Very marvellous it is that Heaven, which really in one sense *is* merciful to sinners, is in no sense merciful to fools, but even lays pitfalls for them, and inevitable snares.

Again and again, in the New Testament, the publican (supposed at once traitor to his country and thief) and the harlot are made the companions of Christ. She out of whom He had cast seven devils, loves Him best, sees Him first, after His resurrection. The sting of that *old* verse, "When thou sawest a thief, thou consentedst to him, and hast been partaker with adulterers," seems done away with. Adultery itself uncondemned,—for, behold, in your hearts is not every one of you alike? "He that is without sin among you, let him first cast a stone at her." And so, and so, no more stones shall be cast nowadays; and here, on the top of our epitaph on the Bishop, lies a notice of the questionable sentence which hanged a man for beating his wife to death with a stick. "The jury recommended him strongly to mercy."

They did so, because they knew not, in their own hearts, what mercy meant. They were afraid to do anything so extremely compromising and disagreeable as causing a man to be hanged,—had no 'pity' for any creatures beaten to death—wives, or beasts; but only a cowardly fear of commanding death, where it was due. Your modern conscience will not incur the responsibility of shortening the hourly more guilty life of a single rogue; but will contentedly fire a salvo of mitrailleuses into a regiment of honest men—leaving Providence to guide the shot. But let us fasten on the word they abused, and understand it. Mercy—misericordia : it does not in the least mean forgiveness of sins,—it means pity of sorrows. In that very instance which the Evangelicals are so fond of quoting—the adultery of David—it is not the Passion for which he is to be judged, but the *want* of Passion,—the want of Pity. *This* he is to judge himself for, by his own mouth :—" As the Lord liveth, the man that hath done this thing shall surely die,—because he hath done this thing, and because he had *no pity.*"

And you will find, alike throughout the record of the Law and the promises of the Gospel, that there is, indeed, forgiveness with God, and Christ, for the passing sins of the hot heart, but none for the eternal and inherent sin of the cold. 'Blessed are the merciful, for they shall obtain mercy' ;—find it you written anywhere that the *un*merciful shall ? ' Her sins, which are many, are forgiven, for she loved much.' But have you record of any one's sins being forgiven who loved not at all ?

I opened my oldest Bible just now, to look for the accurate words of David about the killed lamb ;—a small, closely, and very neatly printed volume it is, printed in Edinburgh by Sir D. Hunter Blair and J. Bruce, Printers to the King's Most Excellent Majesty in 1816. Yellow, now, with age, and flexible, but not unclean, with much use, except that the lower corners of

the pages at 8th of 1st Kings, and 32nd Deutero-
nomy are worn somewhat thin and dark, the learning
of these two chapters having cost me much pains. My
mother's list of the chapters with which, learned every
syllable accurately, she established my soul in life, has
just fallen out of it. And as probably the sagacious
reader has already perceived that these letters are
written in their irregular way, among other reasons, that
they may contain, as the relation may become apposite,
so much of autobiography as it seems to me desirable
to write, I will take what indulgence the sagacious
reader will give me, for printing the list thus accidentally occurrent :—

Exodus,	chapters	15th and 20th.
2 Samuel	„	1st, from 17th verse to the end.
1 Kings	„	8th.
Psalms		23rd, 32nd, 90th, 91st, 103rd, 112th, 119th, 139th
Proverbs	„	2nd, 3rd, 8th, 12th.
Isaiah	„	58th.
Matthew	„	5th, 6th, 7th.
Acts	„	26th.
1 Corinthians	„	13th, 15th.
James	„	4th
Revelation	„	5th, 6th.

And truly, though I have picked up the elements of
a little further knowledge,—in mathematics, meteorology,
and the like, in after life,—and owe not a little to the

teaching of many people, this maternal installation of my mind in that property of chapters, I count very confidently the most precious, and, on the whole, the one essential part of all my education.

For the chapters became, indeed, strictly conclusive and productive to me in all modes of thought ; and the body of divinity they contain, acceptable through all fear or doubt: nor, through any fear or doubt or fault have I ever lost my loyalty to them, nor betrayed the first command in the one I was made to repeat oftenest, " Let not Mercy and Truth forsake Thee."

And at my present age of fifty-five, in spite of some enlarged observations of what modern philosophers call the Reign of Law, I perceive more distinctly than ever the Reign of a Spirit of Mercy and Truth,—infinite in pardon and purification for its wandering and faultful children, who have yet Love in their hearts ; and alto-gether adverse and implacable to its perverse and lying enemies, who have resolute hatred in their hearts, and resolute falsehood on their lips.

This assertion of the existence of a Spirit of Mercy and Truth, as the master first of the Law of Life, and then of the methods of knowledge and labour by which it is sustained, and which the 'Saturday Review' calls the effeminate sentimentality of Mr. Ruskin's poli-tical economy, is accurately, you will observe, reversed by the assertion of the Predatory and Carnivorous—or, in plainer English, flesh-eating spirit in Man himself, as

the regulator of modern civilization, in the paper read
by the Secretary at the Social Science meeting in
Glasgow, 1860. Out of which the following fundamental
passage may stand for sufficient and permanent example
of the existent, practical, and unsentimental English
mind, being the most vile sentence which I have ever
seen in the literature of any country or time :—

"As no one will deny that Man possesses carnivorous
teeth, or that all animals that possess them are more or
less predatory, it is unnecessary to argue, à priori, that a
predatory instinct naturally follows from such organization.
It is our intention here to show how this inevitable
result operates on civilized existence by its being one of
the conditions of Man's nature, and, consequently, of all
arrangements of civilized society."

The paper proceeds, and is entirely constructed, on
the assumption that the predatory spirit is not only one
of the conditions of man's nature, but the particular
condition on which the arrangements of Society are to
be founded. For "Reason would immediately suggest
to one of superior strength, that however desirable it
might be to take possession by violence, of what another had laboured to produce, he might be treated in
the same way by one stronger than himself, to which
he, of course, would have great objection. In order,
therefore, to prevent or put a stop to a practice which
each would object to in his own case," etc., etc. And
so the Social Science interpreter proceeds to sing the

present non-sentimental Proverbs and Psalms of England, —with trumpets also and shawms—and steam whistles. And there is concert of voices and instruments at the Hospital of the Incurabili, and Progress—indubitably—in Chariots of the Night.

NOTES AND CORRESPONDENCE.

———◆———

Corriere dei Bagni.

M'imbarcai su di un vaporetto; era elegante, era vasto, ma il suo contenuto era enormemente superiore al contenente, il vaporetto rigurgitava di uomini, di donne, e di ragazzi.

Il commandante, un fiero giovanotto, gridava: *Montate! Montate!* e la calca si faceva sempre più fitta, ed appena si poteva respirare.

Tutto ad un tratto un sensale di piazza si sentì venir male, e gridò; *io soffoco!* Il commandante si accorse che si soffocava davvero, ed ordino; *basta!*

Il vapore allora si avv ò (*sic*) ed io rimasi stipato fra la folla per diciotto minuti, in capo ai quali ebbi la buona ventura di sbarcare incolume sul pontile dello stabilimento la *Favorita*—Il pontile è lunghissimo, ma elegante e coperto. Il sole per conseguenza non dà nessuna noia.

Una strada che, fino a quando non sia migliorata, non consi glierei di percorrere a chi non abbia i piedi in perfetto stato, con duce al parco della Stabilimento Bagni del signor Delahant —E qui i miei occhi si aprirono per la meraviglia. E diffati, solo una rispettibile forza di volontà ed operosita potè riuscire a tras formare quel luogo, pochi mesi fa ancora deserto ed incolto, in un sito di delisie —Lunghi viali, tappeti erbosi, montagnole, banchine, châlet, strade solitarie e misteriose, lumi, spalti, e poi un interminabile pergolato che conduce allo stabilimento bagni, ed in questo inservienti *vestiti alla marinara,* comodissima vasca, biancheria finissima, e servizio regolare e premuroso.

Sorpreso e contento, mi tuffo allegramente nel mare.

Dopo il bagno è prescritta una passeggiata. Ossequiente ai dettami dell' igiene, riprendo la via e lungo la piacevole spiaggia del mare ritorno alla *Favorita.*

Un châlet, o piuttosto una sala immensa, addobbata con originalità e ricchezza, è divenuta una sala di concerto. Diffatti una eccellente orchestra sta eseguendo pezzi sceltissimi.

Gli artisti indossano tutti la marsina e la cravatta bianca. Ascolto con delizia un *potpourri* del *Faust* e poi torno a girare per il vastissimo parco e visito il *Restaurant.*

Concludeno, il Lido non ha più bisogno di diventare un luogo di delizie, esse lo è in verità diggià diventato, e fra breve i comodi bagni del Lido di Venezia saranno fra i più famosi d'Italia.

Onore ai bravi che hanno operata la meravigliosa trasformazione!

'Il Rinnovamento,' Gazetta del Popolo di Venezia; (2nd July, 1872).

This following part of a useful letter, dated 19th March, 1873, ought to have been printed before now —

"Sir,—Will you permit me to respectfully call your attention to a certain circumstance which has, not unlikely, something to do with the failure (if failure it is) of your appeal for the St. George's Fund?

"At page 22 of Fors Clavigera for May, 1871, your words were, 'Will any such give a tenth of what they have *and* of what they earn?' But in May of the following year, at page 8, the subject is referred to as the giving of 'the tenth of what they have, or make.' The two passages are open to widely differing interpretations. Moreover, none of the sums received appear to have any relation to ' tenths ' either of earnings or possessions.

" Is it not probable that the majority of your readers understood you either to mean literally what you said, or to mean nothing but jest ? They would naturally ask themselves, ' Must it be a tenth of both, or nothing ? ' ' A tenth of either ? ' Or, ' After all, only what we feel able to give ? ' Their perplexity would lead to the giving of nothing. As nobody who has a pecuniary title to ask for an explanation appears to have called your attention to the subject, I, who have no such title, do so now,—feeling impelled thereto by the hint in this month's ' Fors ' of the possible ' non-continuance of the work.'

" May I presume to add one word more ? Last Monday's ' Times ' (March 17th) gave a report of a Working Men's Meeting on the present political crisis. One of the speakers said ' he wanted every working man to be free.' And his idea of freedom he explained to be that all workmen should be at liberty ' to leave their work at a moment's notice.' This, as I have reason to know, is one of the things which working men have got into their heads, and which the newspapers ' get their living by asserting.'

" Lastly, the present English notion of civilizing China by inches, may be worth keeping record of.

" We have Philistines out here, and a Philistine out here is a perfect Goliath. When he imagines that anything is wrong, he says—let it be a Coolie or an Emperor—' Give him a thrashing.' The men of this class here propose their usual remedy ' Let us have a war, and give the Chinese a good licking, and then we shall have the audience question granted, and every thing else will follow.' This includes opening up the country for trade, and civilizing the people, which according to their

theories can be best done by 'thrashing them.' The missionaries
are working to civilize the people here in another way, that
is by the usual plan of tracts and preaching; but their system
is not much in favour, for they make such very small progress
among the 360,000,000, the conversion of which is their
problem. The man of business wants the country opened up
to trade, wants manufactures introduced, the mineral wealth to
be used, and generally speaking the resources of the country
to be developed, 'and that sort of thing, you know—that's
the real way to civilize them.' This, of course, implies a multitu-
dinous breed of Mr. Ruskin's demons, or machinery, to accom-
plish all this. I am here giving the tone of the ideas I hear
expressed around me. It was only the other day that I heard
some of these various points talked over. We were sailing on
the river in a steam launch, which was making the air impure
with its smoke, snorting in a high-pressure way, and whistling
as steam launches are wont to do. The scene was appropriate
to the conversation, for we were among a forest of great junks—
most quaint and picturesque they looked—so old-fashioned they
seemed, that Noah's Ark, had it been there, would have had a
much more modern look about it. My friend, to whom the
launch belonged, and who is in the machinery line himself, gave
his opinion. He began by giving a significant movement of his
head in the direction of the uncouth-looking junks, and then
pointing to his own craft with its engine, said 'he did not
believe much in war, and the missionaries were not of much
account. This is the thing to do it,' he added, pointing to
the launch; 'let us get at them with this sort of article, and
steam at sixty pounds on the square inch; that would soon do
it: that's the thing to civilize them—sixty pounds on the square
inch.'"

FORS CLAVIGERA.

LETTER THE 43rd.

THE CHATEAU-ROUGE. FRENCH FREEDOM

ROME, *Corpus-Domini*, 1874

I WROTE, for a preface to the index at the end of the second volume of Fors, part of an abstract of what had been then stated in the course of this work. Fate would not let me finish it ; but what was done will be useful now, and shall begin my letter for this month. Completing three and a half volumes of Fors, it may contain a more definite statement of its purpose than any given hitherto ; though I have no intention of explaining that purpose entirely, until it is in sufficient degree accomplished. I have a house to build ; but none shall mock me by saying I was not able to finish it, nor be vexed by not finding in it the rooms they expected. But the current and continual purpose of Fors Clavigera is to explain the powers of Chance, or Fortune (Fors), as she offers to men the conditions of prosperity ; and as these conditions are accepted or refused, nails down and fastens their fate for ever, being thus ' Clavigera,'—' nail-bearing.'

The image is one familiar in mythology : my own conception of it was first got from Horace, and developed by steady effort to read history with impartiality, and to observe the lives of men around me with charity. "How you may make your fortune, or mar it," is the expansion of the title.

Certain authoritative conditions of life, of its happiness, and its honour, are therefore stated, in this book, as far as they may be, conclusively and indisputably, at present known I do not enter into any debates, nor advance any opinions.   With what is debateable I am unconcerned ; and when I only have opinions about things, I do not talk about them.   I attack only what cannot on any possible ground be defended ; and state only what I know to be incontrovertibly true.

You will find, as you read Fors more, that it differs curiously from most modern books in this.   Modern fashion is, that the moment a man strikes some little lucifer match, or is hit by any form of fancy, he begins advertising his lucifer match, and fighting for his fancy, totally ignoring the existing sunshine, and the existing substances of things.   But I have no matches to sell, no fancies to fight for.   All that I have to say is that the day is in heaven, and rock and wood on earth, and that you must see by the one, and work with the other.   You have heard as much before, perhaps.   I hope you have ; I should be ashamed if there were anything in Fors which had not been said before,—and that a thousand times, and a thousand times of times,—there is nothing in it, nor ever will be in it, but common truths, as clear to honest mankind as their daily sunrise, as necessary as their daily bread ; and which the fools who deny can only live, themselves, because other men know and obey.

You will therefore find that whatever is set down in Fors for you is assuredly true,—inevitable,—trustworthy to the uttermost,—however strange.* Not because I have any power of knowing more than other people, but simply because I have taken the trouble to ascertain what they also may ascertain if they choose. Compare on this point, Letter VI., page 5.

The following rough abstract of the contents of the first seven letters may assist the reader in their use.

LETTER I. Men's prosperity is in their own hands ; and no forms of government are, in themselves, of the least use. The first beginnings of prosperity must be in getting food, clothes, and fuel. These cannot be got either by the fine arts, or the military arts Neither painting nor fighting feed men ; nor can capital, in the form of money or machinery, feed them. All capital is imaginary or unimportant, except the quantity of food existing in the world

---

* Observe, this is only asserted of its main principles; not of minor and accessory points. I may be entirely wrong in the explanation of a text, or mistake the parish schools of St. Matthias for St. Matthew's, over and over again. I have so large a field to work in that this cannot be helped. But none of these minor errors are of the least consequence to the business in hand.

at any given moment. Finally, men cannot live by lending money to each other, and the conditions of such loan at present are absurd and deadly.*

LETTER II. The nature of Rent. It is an exaction, by force of hand, for the maintenance of Squires but had better at present be left to them. The nature of useful and useless employment. When employment is given by capitalists, it is sometimes useful, but oftener useless ; sometimes moralizing, but oftener demoralizing. And we had therefore better employ ourselves, without any appeal to the capitalists (page 22), and to do this successfully, it must be with three resolutions, namely, to be personally honest, socially helpful, and conditionally obedient (page 23): explained in Letter VII., page 21 to end.

LETTER III. The power of Fate is independent of the Moral Law, but never supersedes it Virtue ceases to be such, if expecting reward . it is therefore never materially rewarded. (I ought to have said, except as one of the appointed means of physical and mental health) The Fates of England, and proper mode of studying them Stories of Henry II. and Richard I

LETTER IV. The value and nature of Education It may be good, bad,—or neither the one nor

---

* See first article in the Notes and Correspondence to this number.

the other. Knowledge is not education, and can neither make us happy nor rich Opening dis_ cussion of the nature and use of riches. Gold and diamonds are not riches, and the reader is challenged to specify their use Opening discussion of the origin of wealth. It does not fall from heaven, (compare Letter VII, page 19,) but is certainly obtainable, and has been generally obtained, by pillage of the poor. Modes in which education in virtue has been made costly to them, and education in vice cheap (Page 23.)

Sir Thomas More's " Utopia."   This letter, though treating of matters necessary to the whole work, yet introduces them prematurely, being written, incidentally, upon the ruin of Paris.

Assisi, 18th May, 1874

So ended, as Fors would have it, my abstraction, which I see Fors had her reason for stopping me in ; else the abstraction would have needed farther abstracting.   As it is, the reader may find in it the real gist of the remaining letters, and discern what a stiff business we have in hand,—rent, capital, and interest, all to be attacked at once ! and a method of education shown to be possible in virtue, as cheaply as in vice !

I should have got my business, stiff though it may be, farther forward by this time, but for that same revolution in Paris, and burning of the Tuileries, which greatly confused my plan by showing me how much baser the human material I had to deal with, was, than I thought in beginning.

That a Christian army (or, at least, one which Saracens would have ranked with that they attacked, under the general name of Franks,) should fiercely devastate and rob an entire kingdom laid at their mercy by the worst distress ;—that the first use made by this distressed country of the defeat of its armies would be to overthrow its government ; and that, when its metropolis had all but perished in conflagration during the contest between its army and mob, no warning should be taken by other civilized societies, but all go trotting on again, next week, in their own several roads to ruin, persistently, as they had trotted before,—bells jingling, and whips cracking,—these things greatly appalled me, finding I had only slime to build with instead of mortar, and shook my plan partly out of shape.

The frightfullest thing of all, to my mind, was the German temper, in its naïve selfishness ; on which point, having been brought round again to it in my last letter, I have now somewhat more to say.

In the 'Pall Mall Gazette' of 7th March, this year, under the head of 'This Evening's News,' appeared an article of which I here reprint the opening portion.

The well-known Hungarian author, Maurus Jokai, is at present a visitor in the German capital. As a man of note he easily obtained access to Prince Bismarck's study, where an interesting conversation took place, which M. Jokai reports pretty fully to the Hungarian journal the *Hon* :—

"The Prince was, as usual, easy in his manner, and communicative, and put a stop at the very outset to the Hungarian's attempt at ceremony. M. Jokai humorously remarked upon the prevalence of 'iron' in the surroundings of the 'iron' Prince. Among other things, there is an iron couch, and an iron safe, in which the Chancellor appears to keep his cigars. Prince Bismarck was struck by the youthful appearance of his guest, who is ten years his junior, but whose writings he remembers to have seen reviewed long ago, in the *Augsburg Gazette* (at that time still, the Chancellor said, a clever paper) when he bore a lieutenant's commission. In the ensuing conversation, Prince Bismarck pointed out the paramount necessity to Europe of a consolidated State in the position of Austro-Hungary. It was mainly on that account that he concluded peace with so great despatch in 1866 Small independent States in the East would be a misfortune to Europe. Austria and Hungary must realize their mutual interdependence, and the necessity of being one. However, the dualist system of government must be preserved, because the task of developing the State, which on this side of the Leitha falls to the Germans, beyond that river naturally falls to the Magyars The notion that Germany has an inclination to annex more land, Prince Bismarck designated as a myth God preserve the Germans from such a wish! Whatever more territory they might acquire would probably be undermined by Papal influence, and they have enough of that already Should the Germans of Austria want to be annexed by Germany, the Chancellor would feel inclined to declare war against them for that wish alone. A German Minister who should conceive the desire to annex part of Austria would deserve to be hanged—a punishment the Prince indicated by gesture He does not wish to annex even a square foot of fresh territory, not as much as two pencils he kept on playing with during the conversation would cover. Those pencils, however, M Jokai remarks, were big enough to serve as walking-sticks, and on the map they would have reached quite from Berlin to Trieste Prince Bismarck went on to justify his annexation of Alsace-Lorraine by geographical necessity. Otherwise he would rather not have grafted the French twig upon the German tree.

The French are enemies never to be appeased. *Take away from them the cook, the tailor, and the hairdresser, and what remains of them is a copper-coloured Indian.*"

Now it does not matter whether Prince Bismarck ever said this, or not. That the saying should be attributed to him in a leading journal, without indication of doubt or surprise, is enough to show what the German temper is publicly recognized to be. And observe what a sentence it is—thus attributed to him. The French are only copper-coloured Indians, finely dressed. This said of the nation which gave us Charlemagne, St Louis, St. Bernard, and Joan of Arc ; which founded the central type of chivalry in the myth of Roland , which showed the utmost height of valour yet recorded in history, in the literal life of Guiscard , and which built Chartres Cathedral !

But the French are not what they were ! No , nor the English, for that matter ; probably we have fallen the farther of the two : meantime the French still retain, at the root, the qualities they always had ; and of one of these, a highly curious and commendable one, I wish you to take some note to-day.

Among the minor nursery tales with which my mother allowed me to relieve the study of the great nursery tale of Genesis, my favourite was Miss Edgeworth's " Frank." The authoress chose this for the boy's name, because she meant him to be a type of Frankness, or openness of heart :—truth of heart, that is to say, *liking* to lay itself open. You are in the habit, I believe, some of you, still, of speaking occasionally of English Frank-ness ,—not recognizing, through the hard clink of the letter K, that you are only talking, all the while, of English Frenchness. Still less when you count your cargoes of gold from San Francisco, do you pause to reflect what San means, or what Francis means, without the Co ,—or how it came to pass that the power of this mountain town of Assisi, where not only no gold can be pug, but where St Francis forbade his Company to dig it anywhere else—came to give names to Devil's towns far across the Atlantic—(and by the way you may note how clumsy the Devil is at christening; for if by chance he gets a fresh York all to himself, he never has any cleverer notion than to call it 'New York'; and in fact, having no mother-wit from his dam, is obliged very often to put up with the old names which were given by Christians,—Nombre di Dios, Trinidad, Vera Cruz, and the like, even when he has all his own way with everything else in the places, but their names).

But to return. You have lately had a fine notion, have you not, of English Liberty as opposed to French Slavery?

Well, whatever your English liberties may be, the French knew what the word meant, before you. For France, if you will consider of it, means nothing else than the Country of Franks;—the country of a race so intensely Free that they for evermore gave name to Freedom. The Greeks sometimes got their own way, as a mob; but nobody, meaning to talk of liberty, calls it 'Greekness.' The Romans knew better what Libertas meant, and their word for it has become common enough, in that straitened form, on your English tongue; but nobody calls it 'Romanness.' But at last comes a nation called the Franks; and they are so inherently free and noble in their natures, that their name becomes the word for the virtue; and when you now want to talk of freedom of heart, you say Frankness, and for the last political privilege which you have it so much in your English minds to get, you haven't so much as an English word, but must call it by the French one, ' Franchise.'*

"Freedom of *heart*," you observe, I say. Not the English freedom of Insolence, according to Mr. B., (see above, Letter 29,) but pure French openness of heart, Fanchette's and her husband's frankness, the source of joy, and courtesy, and civility, and passing softness of human meeting of kindly glance with glance. Of which Franchise, in her own spirit Person, here is the picture for you, from the French Romance of the Rose,— a picture which English Chaucer was thankful to copy.

"And after all those others came Franchise,
Who was not brown, nor grey,   .
But she was white as snow.
And she had not the nose of an Orleanois.
Aussi had she the nose long and straight.
Eyes green, and laughing—vaulted eyebrows ;
She had her hair blonde and long,
And she was simple as a dove.
The body she had sweet, and brightly bred ,
And she dared not do, nor say
To any one, anything she ought not.
And if she knew of any man
Who was in sorrow for love of her,
So soon she had great pity for him,

* See second note at end of this letter.

For she had the heart so pitiful,
And so sweet and so lovely,
That no one suffered pain about her,
But she would help him all she could.
And she wore a surquanye
Which was of no coarse cloth ;
There's none so rich as far as Arras.
And it was so gathered up, and so joined together,
That there was not a single point of it
Which was not set in its exact place, rightly
Much well was dressed Franchise,
For no robe is so pretty
As the surquanye for a demoiselle.
A girl is more gentle and more darling
In surquanye than in coat,
And the white surquanye
Signifies that sweet and frank
Is she who puts it on her."

May I ask you now to take to heart those two lines
of this French description of Frenchness ·

"And she dared not do, nor say
To any one, anything she ought not."

That is not your modern notion of Frenchness, or
franchise, or libertas, or liberty—for all these are syno-
nyms for the same virtue And yet the strange thing
is that the lowest types of the modern French grisette
are the precise corruption of this beautiful Franchise .

and still retain, at their worst, some of the grand old qualities; the absolute sources of corruption being the neglect of their childhood by the upper classes, the abandonment to their own resources, and the development therefore of "Liberty and Independence," in your beautiful English, *not* French, sense.

" Livrée à elle-meme depuis l'âge de treize ans, habituée à ne compter que sur elle seule, elle avait de la vie un expérience dont j'étais confondue. De ce Paris où elle était née, elle savait tout, elle connaissait tout.

Je n'avais pas idée d'une si complète absence de sens moral, d'une si inconsciente dépravation, d'une impudeur si effrontement naive.

La règle de sa conduite, c'était sa fantaisie, son instinct, le caprice du moment.

Elle aimait les longues stations dans les cafés, les mélodrames entremélés de chopines et d'oranges pendant les entr'actes, les parties de canot à Asnières, et surtout, et avant tout, le bal.

Elle était comme chez elle à l'Elysée—Montmartre et au Château-Rouge ; elle y connaissait tout le monde, le chef d'orchestre la saluait, ce dont elle était extraordinairement fière, et quantité de gens la tutoyaient.

Je l'accompagnais partout, dans les commencements, et bien que je n'étais pas précisément naive, ni génée par les scrupules de mon éducation, je fus tellement consternée de l'incroyable désordre de sa vie, que je ne pus m'empêcher de lui en faire quelques représentations.

Elle se fâcha tout rouge.

Tu fais ce qui te plait, me dit–elle, laisse-moi faire ce qui me convient

C'est un justice que je lui dois jamais elle n'essaya sur moi son influence, jamais elle ne m'engagea à suivre son exemple. Ivre de liberté, elle respectait la liberté des autres."

Such is the form which Franchise has taken under republican instruction. But of the true Franchise of Charlemagne and Roland, there were, you must note also, two distinct forms. In the last stanzas of the Chant de Roland, Normandy and France have two distinct epithets,—" Normandie, la franche ; France, la solue" (soluta). "*Frank* Normandy ; *Loose* France." Solute ;—we, adding the dis, use the words loose and dissolute only in evil sense. But 'France la solue ' has an entirely lovely meaning. The frankness of Normandy is the soldier's virtue ; but the unbinding, so to speak, of France, is the peasant's.

> " And having seen that lovely maid,
>   Why should I fear to say
> That she is ruddy, fleet, and strong,
> And down the rocks can leap along
>   Like rivulets in May ? "

It is curious that the most beautiful descriptive line in all Horace,

> " montibus altis
> Levis crepante lympha desilit pede,"

comes in the midst of the dream of the blessed islands which are to be won by following the founders of——what city, think you ?   The city that first sang the "Marseillaise."

"Jupiter illa *piae* secrevit litora genti."

Recollect that line, my French readers, if I chance to find any, this month, nor less the description of those 'arva beata' as if of your own South France ; and then consider also those prophetic lines, true of Paris as of Rome,——

"Nec fera coerulea domuit Germania pube.
Impia, perdemus devoti sanguinis aetas."

Consider them, I say, and deeply, thinking over the full force of those words, "devoti sanguinis," and of the ways in which the pure blood of Normandie la franche, and France la solue, has corrupted itself and become accursed Had I but time to go into the history of that word 'devoveo,' what a piece of philology it would lead us into !   But, for another kind of opposition to the sweet Franchise of old time, take this sentence of description of another French maiden, by the same author from whom I have just quoted the sketch of the grisette :

"C'était une vieille fille d'une cinquantaine d'années, sèche et jaune, avec un grand nez d'oiseau de proie, très noble, encore plus dévote, joueuse comme la dame de pique en personne, et médisante à faire battre des montagnes."

You see what accurate opposition that gives you of

another kind, to Franchise. You even have the 'nez d'Orleanois' specified, which the song of the Rose is so careful to tell you Franchise had not.

Here is another illustrative sentence :

" La colère, à la fin, une de ces terribles colères blanches de dévote, chassait des flots de bile au cerveau de Mademoiselle de la Rochecardeau, et blémissait ses levres."

These three sentences I have taken from two novels of Emilie Gaboriau, " L'argent des autres," and " La Degringolade." They are average specimens of modern French light literature, with its characteristic qualities and defects, and are both of them in many respects worth careful study ; but chiefly in the representation they give, partly with conscious blame, and partly in unconscious corruption, of the Devoti sanguinis aetas ; with which, if you would compare old France accurately, read first Froude's sketch of the life of Bishop Hugo of Lincoln, and think over the scene between him and Cœur de Lion.

You have there, as in life before you, two typical Frenchmen of the twelfth century—a true king, and a true priest, representing the powers which the France of that day contrived to get set over her, and did, on the whole, implicitly and with her heart obey

They are not altogether—by taking the dancing-master and the hairdresser away from them—reduced to copper-coloured Indians.

If, next, you will take the pains—and it will need some pains, for the book is long and occasionally tiresome—to read the Degringolade, you will find it nevertheless worth your while; for it gives you a modern Frenchman's account of the powers which France in the nineteenth century contrived to get set over her, and obeyed—not with her heart, but restively, like an ill-bred dog or mule, which have no honour in their obedience, but bear the chain and bit all the same.

But there is a farther and much more important reason for my wish that you should read this novel. It gives you types of existent Frenchmen and Frenchwomen of a very different class. They are, indeed, only heroes and heroines in a quite second-rate piece of literary work. But these stereotypes, nevertheless, have living originals. There is to be found in France, as truly the Commandant Delorge, as the Comte de Combelaine. And as truly Mademoiselle de Maillefert as the Duchesse de Maumussy. How is it, then, that the Count and Duchess command everything in France, and that the Commandant and Demoiselle command nothing?—that the best they can do is to get leave to live—unknown, and unthought-of? The question, believe me, is for England also, and a very pressing one.

Of the frantic hatred of all religion developed in the French republican mind, the sentences I have quoted are interesting examples. I have not time to speak of them in this letter, but they struck me sharply as I corrected the press to-day; for I had been standing most part of the morning by St. Paul's grave, thinking over his work in the world. A bewildered peasant, from some green dingle of Campagna, who had seen me kneel when the Host passed, and took me therefore to be a human creature and a friend, asked me 'where St. Paul was'?

'There, underneath,' I answered

'There?' he repeated, doubtfully,—as dissatisfied.

'Yes,' I answered; 'his body at least;—his head is at the Lateran.'

'Il suo corpo,' again he repeated, still as in discontent. Then, after a pause, 'E la sua statua?'

Such a wicked thing to ask for that! wasn't it, my Evangelical friends? You would so much rather have had him ask for Hudson's!

NOTES AND CORRESPONDENCE.

I. I have had by me, some time, three eager little fragments from one of Mr. Sillar's letters:—*too* eager, always, in thinking this one sin of receiving interest on money means every other. I know many excellent people, happily, whose natures have not been spoiled by it: the more as it has been done absolutely without knowledge of being wrong. I did not find out the wrong of it myself, till Mr. Sillar showed me the way to judge of it.

The passage which I have italicized, from Mr. Lecky, is a very precious statement of his sagacious creed. The chief jest of it is his having imagined himself to *be* of Aristotle's ' species '!

" To get profit without responsibility has been a fond scheme as impossible of honest attainment as the philosopher's stone or perpetual motion. Visionaries have imagined such things to exist, but it has been reserved for this mammon-worshipping generation to find it in that arrangement by which a man, without labour, can secure a permanent income with perfect security, and without diminution of the capital.

" A view of it is evidently taken by Lord Bacon when he says that usury bringeth the treasure of a realm into few hands; for the usurer trading on a certainty, and other men on uncertainties, at the end of the game all the money will be in the box.

" We have had now an opportunity of practically testing this theory; not more than seventeen years have elapsed since all restraint was removed from the growth of what Lord Coke calls this 'pestilent weed,' and we see Bacon's words verified, the rich becoming richer, and the poor poorer, is the cry throughout the whole civilized world.   Rollin in his Ancient History, speaking of the Roman Empire, tells us that it has been the ruin of every state where it was tolerated.   It is in a fair way to ruin this of ours, and ruin it it will, unless England's sons calmly and candidly investigate the question for themselves, and resolutely act upon the conclusions to which the investigation must lead them.

" There is such a thing as unlimited liability; of the justice of such laws I do not now speak, but the law exists, and as it was made by moneyed men in the interest of moneyed men they cannot refuse to be judged by it.   The admission, therefore, of the fact that interest is a share of the profit, would throw upon the money-lender the burden of unlimited liability; this he certainly refuses to admit, consequently he has no alternative but to confess that interest has nothing whatever to do with profit, but that it is a certain inherent property of money, viz., that of producing money, and that interest is as legitimately the offspring of money as a Calf is that of a Cow.   That this is really the stand now taken, may be shown from the literature and practice of the present day.   Mr. Lecky, one of the latest champions of interest, boldly admits it.   In his history of the rise and influence of rationalism in Europe, p. 284, after quoting Aristotle's saying, that all money is sterile by nature, he says, ' *This is an absurdity of Aristotle's, and the number of centuries during which it was incessantly asserted without being (so far as we know) once questioned, is a curious illustration of the longevity of a sophism when expressed in a terse form, and sheltered by a great name.   It is enough to make one ashamed of his species to think that Bentham was the first to bring into notice the simple consideration that if the borrower employs the borrowed money in buying bulls and cows, and if these produce calves to ten times the value of the interest, the money borrowed can scarcely be said to be sterile.'*

" And now to remedy all this. Were there no remedy, to parade it in our view, would be cruel; but there is one, so simple, that like those of divine making, it may be despised for its simplicity. It consists in the recognition of the supreme wisdom which forbade the taking of usury. We should not reimpose the usury laws, which were in themselves a blunder and a snare, nor would we advocate the forcible repression of the vice any more than we do that of other vices, such as gambling or prostitution, but we would put them on precisely the same footing, and enact thus—

Whereas, usury is a sin detestable and abominable, the law will refuse to recognize any contract in which it is an element.

The first effect of this would be, that all those who had lent, taking security into their hands, would have no power of oppression beyond keeping the pledge,—the balance of their debts being on a similar footing to those of the men who had lent without security.

" To these their chance of repayment would depend on their previous conduct. If they had lent their money to honourable men, they would surely be repaid; if to rogues, they surely would not; and serve them right. Those, and those only, who have lent without interest would have the power of an action at law to recover. and as such men must have possessed philanthropy, they could safely be trusted with that power.

" Regarding the future employment of money, a usurer who intended to continue his unholy trade, would lend only to such men as would repay without legal pressure, and from such men trade would not have to fear competition. But to disreputable characters the money-market would be hermetically sealed, and then as commerce, freed from the competition of these scoundrels, began again to be remunerative, we should find it more to our advantage to take an interest *in* commerce than usury *from* it, and so gradually would equity supersede iniquity, and peace and prosperity be found where now abound corruption, riot, and rebellion, with all the host of evils inseparable from a condition of plethoric wealth on one hand, and on the other hopeless and despairing poverty."

II. I intended in this note to have given some references to the first use of the word Franc, as an adjective. But the best dictionary-makers seem to have been foiled by it. "I recollect," (an Oxford friend writes to me,) "Clovis called his axe 'Francisca' when he threw it to determine by its fall where he should build a church," and in Littre's dictionary a root is suggested, in the Anglo-Saxon Franca, 'javelin.' But I think these are all collateral, not original uses. I am not sure even when the word came to be used for the current silver coin of France that, at least, must be ascertainable. It is curious that in no fit of Liberty and Equality, the anti-Imperialists have thought of calling their golden coins 'Citizens' instead of 'Napoleons' nor even their sous, Sansculottes.

III. Some of my correspondents ask me what has become of my promised additional Fors on the glaciers. Well, it got crevassed, and split itself into three; and then relegated itself into a somewhat compact essay on glaciers; and then got jammed up altogether, because I found that the extremely scientific Professor Tyndall had never distinguished the quality of viscosity from plasticity, (or the consistence of honey from that of butter,) still less the gradations of character in the approach of metals, glass, or stone, to their freezing-points; and that I wasn't as clear as could be wished on some of these matters myself, and, in fact, that I had better deal with the subject seriously in my Oxford lectures than in Fors, which

I hope to do this next autumn, after looking again at the riband structure of the Brenva Meantime, here—out of I don't know what paper, (I wish my correspondents would always *cross* the slips they cut out with the paper's name and date,)—is a lively account of the present state of affairs, with a compliment to Professor Tyndall on his style of debate, which I beg humbly to endorse.

"An awful battle, we regret to say, is now raging between some of the most distinguished men of Science, Literature, and Art, for all those three fair sisters have hurtled into the Homeric fray. The combatants on one side are Professors G. Forbes, Tait, and Ruskin, with Mr. Alfred Wills, and on the other— alone, but fearless and undismayed—the great name of Tyndall. The *causa teterrima belli* is in itself a cold and unlikely one— namely, the glaciers of Switzerland; but fiercer the fight could not be, we grieve to state, if the question of eternal punishment, with all its fiery accessory scenery, were under discussion. We have no rash intention of venturing into that terrible battle- ground where Professor Ruskin is laying about him with his ' Fors Clavigera,' and where Professor Tait, like another Titan, hurls wildly into the affrighted air such epithets as ' con- temptible,' ' miserable,' ' disgusting,' ' pernicious,' ' pestilent.' These adjectives, for anything that ignorant journalists can know, may mean, in Scotch scientific parlance, everything that is fair, chivalrous, becoming, and measured in argument. But, merely from the British instinct of fair play, which does not like to see four against one, and without venturing a single word about the glaciers, we cannot help remarking how much more consistent with the dignity of science appears Professor Tyndall's answer in the last number of the *Contemporary Review* If it be true that the man who keeps his temper is generally in the right, we shall decidedly back Mr. Tyndall and the late lamented Agassiz in the present dreadful conflict. Speaking, for instance, of those same furious adjectives, which we have culled from the literary parterre of Professor Tait, Dr. Tyndall sweetly says, 'The spirit which prompts them may, after all, be but a local distortion of that noble force of heart which answered the Cameron's Gathering at Waterloo; carried the Black Watch to Coomassie, and which has furnished Scotland with the materials of an immortal history. Still, rudeness is not independence, bluster is not strength, nor is coarseness courage. We have won the human understanding from the barbarism of the past; but we have won along with it the dignity, courtesy, and truth of civilized life. And the man who on the platform or in the press does violence to this ethical side of human nature discharges but an imperfect duty to the public, whatever the qualities of his understanding may be.' This, we humbly think, is how men of science ought to talk when they quarrel—if they quarrel at all."

I hope much to profit by this lesson. I have not my "School for Scandal" by me—but I know where to find it the minute I get home; and I'll do my best. "The man who," etc., etc. ;—yes, I think I can manage it.

FORS CLAVIGERA.

LETTER THE 44th.

THE SQUIRREL CAGE

ENGLISH SERVITUDE

ROME, *6th June,* 1874

THE poor Campagna herdsman, whose seeking for St Paul's statue the Professor of Fine Art in the University of Oxford so disgracefully failed to assist him in, had been kneeling nearer the line of procession of the Corpus Domini than I ;—in fact, quite among the rose-leaves which had been strewed for a carpet round the aisles of the Basilica. I grieve to say that I was shy of the rose-bestrewn path, myself ; for the crowd waiting at the side of it had mixed up the rose-leaves with spittle so richly as to make quite a pink pomatum of them. And, indeed, the living temples of the Holy Ghost which in any manner bestir themselves here among the temples,—whether of Roman gods or Christian saints,—have merely and simply the two great operations upon them of filling their innermost adyta with dung, and making their pavements slippery with spittle ; the Pope's new tobacco manufactory under the Palatine,—an infinitely more important object now, in all views of Rome from the west, than either the Palatine or the Capitol,—greatly aiding and encouraging this especial form of lustration : while the still more ancient documents of Egyptian religion—the obelisks of the Piazza del Popolo, and of the portico of St. Peter's—are entirely eclipsed by the obelisks of our English religion, lately elevated, in full view from the Pincian and the Montorio, with smoke coming out of the top of them. And farther, the entire eastern district of Rome, between the two Basilicas of the Lateran and St. Lorenzo, is now one mass of volcanic ruin ;—a desert of dust and ashes, the lust of wealth exploding there, out of a crater deeper than Etna's, and raging, as far as it can reach, in one frantic desolation of whatever is lovely, or holy, or memorable, in the central city of the world.

For there is one fixed idea in the mind of every European progressive politician, at this time ; namely, that by a certain application of Financial Art, and by the erection of a certain quantity of new buildings on a colossal scale, it will be possible for society hereafter to pass its entire life in eating, smoking, harlotry, and talk ; without doing anything whatever with its hands or feet of a laborious character. And as these new buildings, whose edification is a main article of this modern political faith and hope,—(being required for gambling and dining in on a large scale),—cannot be raised without severely increased taxation of the poorer classes, (here in Italy direct, and in all countries consisting in the rise of price in all articles of food—wine alone in Italy costing just ten times what it did ten years ago,) and this increased taxation and distress are beginning to be felt too grievously to be denied ; nor only so, but—which is still less agreeable to modern politicians—with slowly dawning perception of their true causes,—one finds also the popular journalists, for some time back addressing themselves to the defence of Taxation, and Theft in general, after this fashion.

" The wealth in the world may practically be regarded as infinitely great. It is not true that what one man appropriates becomes thereupon useless to others, and it is also untrue that force or fraud, direct or indirect, are the principal, or, indeed, that they are at all common or important, modes of acquiring wealth."—*Pall Mall Gazette*, Jan. 14th, 1869.*

---

* The passage continues thus, curiously enough,—for the parallel of the boat at sea is precisely that which I have given, in *true* explanation of social phenomena :—

" The notion that when one man becomes rich he makes others poor, will be found upon examination to depend upon the assumption that there is in the world a fixed quantity of wealth ; that when one man appropriates to himself a large amount of it, he excludes all others from any benefit arising from it, and that at the same time he forces some one else to be content with less than he would otherwise have had. Society, in short, must be compared to a boat at sea, in which there is a certain quantity of fresh water, and a certain number of shipwrecked passengers. In that case, no doubt, the water drunk by one is of no use to

The philosophical journalist, after some further contemptuous statement of the vulgar views on this subject, conveniently dispenses (as will be seen by reference to the end of the clause in the note) with the defence of his own. I will undertake the explanation of what was, perhaps, even to himself, not altogether clear in his impressions. If a burglar ever carries off the Editor's plate-basket, the bereaved Editor will console himself by reflecting that " it is not true that what one man appropriates becomes thereupon useless to others : "—for truly (he will thus proceed to finer investigation,) this plate of mine, melted down, after being transitionally serviceable to the burglar, will enter again into the same functions among the silver of the world which it had in my own possession ; so that the intermediate benefit to the burglar may be regarded as entirely a form of trade profit, and a kind of turning over of capital. And " it is also untrue that force or fraud, direct or indirect, are the principal, or indeed that they are at all common or important, modes of acquiring wealth,"—for this poor thief, with his crowbar and jemmy, does but disfurnish my table for a day , while I, with my fluent pen, can replenish it any number

---

the rest, and if one drinks more, others must drink less, as the water itself is a fixed quantity. Moreover, no one man would be able to get more than a rateable share, except by superior force, or by some form of deceit, because the others would prevent him. The mere statement of this view ought to be a sufficient exposure of the fundamental error of the commonplaces which we are considering."

of times over, by the beautiful expression of my opinions for the public benefit. But what manner of fraud, or force, there may be in living by the sale of one's opinions, instead of knowledges , and what quantity of true knowledge on any subject whatsoever—moral, political, scientific, or artistic—forms at present the total stock in trade of the Editors of the European Press, our Pall Mall Editor has very certainly not considered.

" The wealth in the world practically infinite,"—is it ? Then it seems to me, the poor may ask, with more reason than ever before, Why have we not our share of Infinity ? We thought, poor ignorants, that we were only the last in the scramble , we submitted, believing that somebody must be last, and somebody first. But if the mass of good things be inexhaustible, and there are horses for everybody,—why is not every beggar on horseback ? And, for my own part, why should the question be put to me so often,—which I am sick of answering and answering again,—" How, with our increasing population, are we to live without Machinery ? " For if the wealth be already infinite, what need of machinery to make more ? Alas, if it *could* make more, what a different world this might be Arkwright and Stephenson would deserve statues indeed,—as much as St. Paul. If all the steam engines in England, and all the coal in it, with all their horse and ass power put together, could produce—so much as one grain of corn ! The last time this perpetually recurring question about machinery was asked me, it was very earnestly and candidly pressed, by a master manufacturer, who honestly desired to do in his place what was serviceable to England, and honourable to himself. I answered at some length, in private letters, of which I asked and obtained his leave to print some parts in Fors. They may as well find their place in this number; and for preface to them, here is a piece, long kept by me, concerning railroads, which may advisably now be read.

Of modern machinery for locomotion, my readers, I suppose, thought me writing in ill-temper, when I said in one of the letters on the childhood of Scott, "infernal means of locomotion"? Indeed, I am always compelled to write, as always compelled to live, in ill-temper. But I never set down a single word but with the serenest purpose. I *meant* "infernal" in the most perfect sense the word will bear.

For instance. The town of Ulverstone is twelve miles from me, by four miles of mountain road beside Coniston lake, three through a pastoral valley, five by the seaside. A healthier or lovelier walk would be difficult to find.

In old times, if a Coniston peasant had any business at Ulverstone, he walked to Ulverstone; spent nothing but shoe-leather on the road, drank at the streams, and if he spent a couple of batz when he got to Ulverstone, "it was the end of the world." But now, he would never think of doing such a thing! He first walks three miles in a contrary direction, to a railroad station, and then travels by railroad twenty-four miles to Ulverstone, paying two shillings fare. During the twenty-four miles transit, he is idle, dusty, stupid ; and either more hot or cold than is pleasant to him. In either case he drinks beer at two or three of the stations, passes his time, between them, with anybody he can find, in talking without having anything to talk of; and such talk always becomes vicious. He arrives at Ulverstone, jaded, half drunk, and otherwise demoralized, and three shillings, at least, poorer than in the morning. Of that sum a shilling has gone for beer, threepence to a railway shareholder, threepence in coals, and eighteenpence has been spent in employing strong men in the vile mechanical work of making and driving a machine, instead of his own legs, to carry the drunken lout. The results, absolute loss and demoralization to the poor, on all sides, and iniquitous gain to the rich. Fancy, if you saw the railway officials actually employed in carrying the countryman bodily on their backs to Ulverstone, what you would think of the business ! And because they waste ever so much iron and fuel besides to do it, you think it a profitable one !

And for comparison of the advantages of old times and new, for travellers of higher order, hear how Scott's excursions used to be made.

" Accordingly, during seven successive years, Scott made a raid, as he called it, into Liddesdale, with Mr.

Shortreed for his guide, exploring every rivulet to its source, and every ruined peel from foundation to battlement At this time no wheeled carriage had ever been seen in the district ; the first, indeed, that ever appeared there was a gig, driven by Scott himself for a part of his way, when on the last of these seven excursions. There was no inn *nor public-house of any kind* in the whole valley ; the travellers passed from the shepherd's hut to the minister's manse, and again from the cheerful hospitality of the manse to the rough and jolly welcome of the homestead ; gathering, wherever they went, songs and tunes, and occasionally more tangible relics of antiquity—even such 'a rowth of auld nicknackets' as Burns ascribes to Captain Grose. To these rambles Scott owed much of the materials of his 'Minstrelsy o' the Scottish Border'; and not less of that intimate acquaintance with the living manners of these unsophisticated regions, which constitutes the chief charm of the most charming of his prose works. But how soon he had any definite object before him in his researches seems very doubtful. ' He was makin' himsel' a' the time,' said Mr. Shortreed , 'but he didna ken maybe what he was about, till years had passed. At first he thought o' little, I dare say, but the queerness and the fun.'

' It was that same season, I think,' says Mr. Shortreed, 'that Sir Walter got from Dr. Elliot the large old border war horn, which ye may still see hanging in the armoury at Abbotsford. How great he was when he

was made master o' that! I believe it had been found
in Hermitage Castle—and one of the doctor's servants
had used it many a day as a grease-horn for his scythe
before they had discovered its history. When cleaned
out, it was never a hair the worse ; the original chain,
hoop, and mouthpiece of steel were all entire, just as
you now see them. Sir Walter carried it home all the
way from Liddesdale to Jedburgh slung about his neck
like Johnny Gilpin's bottle, while I was entrusted with
an ancient bridle-bit, which we had likewise picked up.

   " ' The feint o' pride—nae pride had he, . .

    A lang kail-gully hung down by his side,

    And a great meikle nowt-horn to rout on had he.'

And meikle and sair we routed on't, and ' hotched and
blew wi' micht and main.' O what pleasant days ! and
then *a' the nonsense we had cost us nothing. We never
put hand in pocket* for a week on end. Toll-bars there
were none, and indeed I think our haill charges were a
feed o' corn to our horses in the gangin' and comin' at
Riccartoun mill.' "

This absolute economy,* of course, could only exist
when travelling was so rare that patriarchal hospitality
could still be trusted for its lodging. But the hospitality

---

* The reader might at first fancy that the economy was not " absolute,"
but that the expenses of the traveller were simply borne by his host Not
so ; the host only gave what he in his turn received, when he also travelled.
Every man thus carried his home with him, and to travel. was merely to walk
or ride from place to place, instead of round one's own house. (See Saunders
Fairford's expostulation with Alan on the charges incurred at Noble House)

of the inn need not be less considerate or true because the inn's master lives in his occupation. Even in these days, I have had no more true or kind friend than the now dead Mrs. Eisenkraemer of the *old* Union Inn at Chamouni ; and an innkeeper's daughter in the Oberland taught me that it was still possible for a Swiss girl to be refined, imaginative, and pure-hearted, though she waited on her father's guests, and though these guests were often vulgar and insolent English travellers. For she had been bred in the rural districts of happy olden days,— to which, as it chances, my thoughts first turned, in the following answer to my English manufacturing friend.

On any given farm in Switzerland or Bavaria, fifty years ago, the master and his servants lived, in abundance, on the produce of their ground, without machinery, and exchanged some of its surplus produce for Lyons velvet and Hartz silver, (produced by the unhappy mechanists and miners of those localities,) whereof the happy peasant made jackets and bodices, and richly adorned the same with precious chain-work. It is not more than ten years since I saw in a farm-shed near Thun, three handsome youths and three comely girls, all in well-fitting, pretty, and snow-white shirt and chemisette, threshing corn with a steady shower of timed blows, as skilful in their—cadence, shall we, literally, say ?—as the most exquisitely performed music, and as rapid as its swiftest notes. There was no question for any of them, whether they should have their dinner when they had earned it, nor the slightest chance of any of them going in rags through the winter.

That is entirely healthy, happy, and wise human life Not a theoretical or Utopian state at all; but one which over large districts of the world has long existed, and must, thank God, in spite of British commerce and its consequences, for ever, somewhere, exist.

But the farm, we will say, gets over-populous, (it always does, of course, under ordinary circumstances,) that is to say, the ground no longer affords corn and milk enough for the people on it. Do you suppose you will make more of the corn, because you now thresh it with a machine? So far from needing to do so, you have more hands to employ than you had—can have twelve flails going instead of six. You make your twelve human creatures stand aside, and thresh your corn with a steam engine. You gain time, do you? What's the use of time to you? did it not hang heavy enough on your hands before? You thresh your entire farm produce, let us say, in twelve minutes. Will that make it one grain more, to feed the twelve mouths? Most assuredly, the soot and stench of your steam engine will make your crop *less* next year, but not one grain more can you have to-day.* But you don't mean to use your engines to thresh with or plough with? Well,

* But what is to be done, then? Emigrate, of course; but under different laws from those of modern emigration. Don't emigrate to China, poison Chinamen, and teach them to make steam engines, and then import Chinamen, to dig iron *here.* But see next Fors

that is one point of common sense gained. What will you do with them, then ?—spin and weave cotton, sell the articles you manufacture, and buy food ? Very good ; then somewhere there must be people still living as *you* once did,—that is to say, producing more corn and milk than they want, and able to give it to you in exchange for your cotton, or velvet, or what not, which you weave with your steam. Well, *those* people, wherever they are, and whoever they may be, are your lords and masters thenceforth. *They* are living happy and wise human lives, and are served by you, their mechanics and slaves. Day after day your souls will become more mechanical, more servile : also you will go on multiplying, wanting more food, and more ; you will have to sell cheaper and cheaper, work longer and longer, to buy your food. At last, do what you can, you can make no more, or the people who have the corn will not want any more , and your increasing population will necessarily come to a quite imperative stop — by starvation, preceded necessarily by revolution and massacre.

And now examine the facts about England in this broad light.

She has a vast quantity of ground still food-producing, in corn, grass, cattle, or game. With that territory she educates her squire, or typical gentleman, and his tenantry, to whom, together, she owes all her power in the world. With another large portion of territory,—now continually on the increase,—she educates a mercenary population, ready to produce any quantity of bad articles to anybody's order ; population which every hour that passes over them makes acceleratingly avaricious, immoral, and insane. In the increase of that kind of territory and its people, her ruin is just as certain as if she were deliberately exchanging her corn-growing land, and her heaven above it, for a soil of arsenic, and rain of nitric acid.

" Have the Arkwrights and Stephensons, then, done nothing but harm ? " Nothing ; but the root of all the mischief is not in Arkwrights or Stephensons ; nor in rogues or mechanics. The real root of it is the crime of the squire himself. And the method of that crime is thus A certain quantity of the food produced by the country is paid annually by it into the squire's hand, in the form of rent, privately, and taxes, publicly. If he uses this food to support a food-producing population, he increases daily the strength of the country and his own ; but if he uses it to support an idle population, or one producing merely trinkets in iron, or gold, or other rubbish, he steadily weakens the country, and debases himself.

Now the action of the squire for the last fifty years has been, broadly, to take the food from the ground of his estate, and carry it to London, where he feeds with it* a vast number of builders, upholsterers, (one

* The writings of our vulgar political economists, calling money only a " medium of exchange," blind the foolish public conveniently to all the practical actions of the machinery of the currency. Money is not a medium of exchange, but a token of right. I have, suppose, at this moment. ten, twenty, or thirty thousand pounds That signifies that. as compared with a man who has only ten pounds, I can claim possession of, call for, and do

of them charged me five pounds for a footstool the other day,) carriage and harness makers, dress-makers, grooms, footmen, bad musicians, bad painters, gamblers, and harlots, and in supply of the wants of these main classes, a vast number of shopkeepers of minor useless articles The muscles and the time of this enormous population being wholly unproductive—(for of course time spent in the mere process of sale is unproductive, and much more that of the footman and groom, while that of the vulgar upholsterer, jeweller, fiddler, and painter, etc., etc., is not only unproductive, but mischievous,)—the entire mass of this London population do nothing whatever either to feed or clothe themselves ; and their vile life preventing them from all rational entertainment, they are compelled to seek some pastime in a vile literature, the demand for which again occupies another enormous class, who do nothing to feed or dress themselves ; finally, the vain disputes of this vicious population give employment to the vast industry of the lawyers and their clerks,* who similarly do nothing to feed or dress themselves.

what I like with a thousand, or two thousand, or three thousand times as much of the valuable things existing in the country The peasant accordingly gives the squire a certain number of these tokens or counters, which give the possessor a right to claim so much corn or meat The squire gives these tokens to the various persons in town, enumerated in the text, who then claim the corn and meat from the peasant, returning him the counters, which he calls " price," and gives to the squire again next year.

* Of the industry of the Magistrate against crime, I say nothing ; for it now scarcely exists, but to do evil See first article in Correspondence, at end of letter

Now the peasants might still be able to supply this enormous town population with food, (in the form of the squire's rent,) but it cannot, without machinery, supply the flimsy dresses, toys, metal work, and other rubbish, belonging to their accursed life. Hence over the whole country the sky is blackened and the air made pestilent, to supply London and other such towns * with their iron railings, vulgar upholstery, jewels, toys, liveries, lace, and other means of dissipation and dishonour of life. Gradually the country people cannot even supply food to the voracity of the vicious centre ; and it is necessary to import food from other countries, giving in exchange any kind of commodity we can attract their itching desires for, and produce by machinery. The tendency of the entire national energy is therefore to approximate more and more to the state of a squirrel in a cage, or a turnspit in a wheel, fed by foreign masters with nuts and dog's-meat. And indeed, when we rightly conceive the relation of London to the country, the sight of it becomes more fantastic and wonderful than any dream Hyde Park, in the season, is the great rotatory form of the vast squirrel-cage ; round and round it go the idle company, in their reversed streams, urging themselves to their necessary exercise They cannot with safety even eat their nuts, without so much 'revolution' as shall, in Venetian language,

* Compare, especially, Letter xxix , p 11

'comply with the demands of hygiene.' Then they re-
tire into their boxes, with due quantity of straw ; the
Belgravian and Piccadillian streets outside the railings
being, when one sees clearly, nothing but the squirrel's
box at the side of his wires. And then think of all
the rest of the metropolis as the creation and ordinance
of these squirrels, that they may squeak and whirl
to their satisfaction, and yet be fed. Measure the
space of its entirely miserable life. Begin with that
diagonal which I struck from Regent Circus to Drury
Lane ; examine it, house by house ; then go up from
Drury Lane to St Giles' Church, look into Church Lane
there, and explore your Seven Dials and Warwick Street ;
and remember this is the very centre of the mother
city,—precisely between its Parks, its great Library and
Museum, its principal Theatres, and its Bank. Then
conceive the East-end , and the melancholy Islington and
Pentonville districts ; then the ghastly spaces of southern
suburb—Vauxhall, Lambeth, the Borough, Wapping, and
Bermondsey. All this is the nidification of those Park
Squirrels. This is the thing they have produced round
themselves ; this their work in the world. When they
rest from their squirrellian revolutions, and die in the
Lord, and their works do follow them, *these* are what
will follow them. Lugubrious march of the Waterloo
Road, and the Borough, and St. Giles's ; the shadows of
all the Seven Dials having fetched their last compass.
New Jerusalem, prepared as a bride, of course, opening

her gates to them ;—but, pertinaciously attendant, Old Jewry outside. " Their works do follow them."

For these streets are indeed what they have built ; their inhabitants the people they have chosen to educate. They took the bread and milk and meat from the people of their fields ; they gave it to feed, and retain here in their service, this fermenting mass of unhappy human beings,—news-mongers, novel-mongers, picture-mongers, poison-drink-mongers, lust and death-mongers ; the whole smoking mass of it one vast dead-marine storeshop,—accumulation of wreck of the Dead Sea, with every activity in it, a form of putrefaction.

Some personal matters were touched upon in my friend's reply to this letter, and I find nothing more printable of the correspondence but this following fragment or two.

" But what are you to do, having got into this mechanical line of life ? "

You must persevere in it, and do the best you can for the present, but resolve to get out of it as soon as may be. The one essential point is to know thoroughly that it is wrong ; how to get out of it, you can decide afterwards, at your leisure.

" But somebody must weave by machinery, and dig in mines : else how could one have one's velvet and silver chains ? "

Whatever machinery is needful for human purposes can be driven by wind or water ; the Thames alone could drive mills enough to weave velvet and silk for all England.   But even mechanical occupation not involving pollution of the atmosphere must be as limited as possible , for it invariably degrades.   You may use your slave in your silver mine, or at your loom, to avoid such labour yourself, if you honestly believe you have brains to be better employed ,—or you may yourself, for the service of others, honourably *become* their slave ; and, in benevolent degradation, dig silver or weave silk, making yourself semi-spade, or semi-worm   But you must not eventually, for no purpose or motive whatsoever, live amidst smoke and filth, nor allow others to do so , you must see that your slaves are as comfortable and safe as their employment permits, and that they are paid wages high enough to allow them to leave it often for redemption and rest.

Eventually, I say ; how fast events may move, none of us know ; in our compliance with them, let us at least be intelligently patient—if at all ; not blindly patient.

For instance, there is nothing really more monstrous in any recorded savagery or absurdity of mankind, than that governments should be able to get money for any folly they choose to commit, by selling to capitalists the right of taxing future generations to the end of time   All the cruellest wars inflicted, all the basest luxuries grasped by the idle classes, are thus paid for by the poor a hundred times over. And yet I am obliged to keep my money in the funds or the bank, because I know no other mode of keeping it safe ; and if I refused to take the interest, I should only throw it into the hands of the very people who would use it for these evil purposes, or, at all events, for less good than I can. Nevertheless it is daily becoming a more grave question with me what it may presently be right to do. It may be better to diminish private charities, and much more, my own luxury of life, than to comply in any sort with a national sin. But I am not agitated or anxious in the matter : content to know my principle, and to work steadily towards better fulfilment of it.

And this is all that I would ask of my correspondent or of any other man,—that he should know what he is about, and be steady in his line of advance or retreat I know myself to be an usurer as long as I take interest on any money whatsoever. I confess myself such, and abide whatever shame or penalty may attach to usury, until I can withdraw myself from the system. So my correspondent says he must abide by his post. I think so too. A naval captain, though I should succeed in persuading him of the wickedness of war, would in like manner, if he were wise, abide at his post ; nay, would be entirely traitorous and criminal if he at once deserted it. Only let us all be sure what our positions are ; and if, as it is said, the not living by interest and the resolutely making everything as good as can be, are incompatible with the present state of society, let us, though compelled to remain usurers and makers of bad things, at least not deceive ourselves as to the nature of our acts and life.

Leaving thus the personal question, how the great courses of life are to be checked or changed, to each man's conscience and discretion,—this following answer I would make in all cases to the inquiry, 'What can I *do?*'

If the present state of this so-called rich England is so essentially miserable and poverty-stricken that honest men must always live from hand to mouth, while speculators make fortunes by cheating them out of their labour, and if, therefore, no sum can be set aside for charity,—the paralyzed honest men can certainly do little for the present. But, with what can be spared for charity, if *anything*, do this; buy ever so small a bit of ground, in the midst of the worst back deserts of our manufacturing towns; six feet square, if no more can be had,—nay, the size of a grave, if you will, but buy it *freehold*, and make a garden of it, by hand-labour, a garden visible to all men, and cultivated *for* all men of that place. If absolutely nothing will grow in it, then have herbs carried there in pots Force the bit of ground into order, cleanliness, *green* or *coloured* aspect. What difficulties you have in doing this are your best subjects of thought; the good you will do in doing this, the best in your present power.

What the best in your ultimate power may be, will
depend on the action of the English landlord ; for
observe, we have only to separate the facts of the Swiss
farm to ascertain what they are with respect to any state.
We have only to ask what quantity of food it produces,
how much it exports in exchange for other articles, and
how much it imports in exchange for other articles. The
food-producing countries have the power of educating
gentlemen and gentlewomen if they please,—they are
the lordly and masterful countries. Those which exchange mechanical or artistic productions for food are
servile, and necessarily in process of time will be ruined.
Next Fors, therefore, will be written for any Landlords
who wish to be true Workmen in their vocation , and,
according to the first law of the St. George's Company,
' to do good work, whether they die or live.'

NOTES AND CORRESPONDENCE.

I commend the whole of the following letter to the reader's most serious consideration —

BROXBOURN, HERTS, 11*th June*, 1874.

My dear Sir,—You are so tolerant of correspondents with grievances, that I venture to say a few more words, in reply to your note about Law Reform. In November next the Judicature Bill will come into operation. The preamble recites this incontestable fact, "that it is expedient to make provision for the better administration of justice in England." Now, the two salient features of the incessant clamour for Law Reform are these—1st, an increased conviction of the sanctity of property; 2nd, a proportionate decrease in the estimate of human life. For years past the English people have spent incalculable money and talk in trying to induce Parliament to give them safe titles to their land, and sharp and instant means of getting in their debts : the Land Transfer Bill is in answer to this first demand, and the Judicature Bill to the second. Meanwhile the Criminal Code may shift for itself, and here we have, as the outcome of centuries of vulgar national flourish about Magna Charta, Habeas Corpus, and much else, the present infamous system of punishing crime by pecuniary penalties. Now the spirit of this evil system is simply this : " A crime is an offence against society. Making the criminal suffer pain won't materially benefit society, but making him suffer in his pocket *will;*" and so society elects to be battered about, and variously maltreated, on a sliding scale of charges, adjusted more on medical than moral principles. No doubt it is very desirable to have a title-deed to your thousand acres, no bigger than the palm of your hand, to be able to put it in a box, and sit upon it, and defy all the lawyers in the land to pick a flaw in your title ; quite a millennium-like state of things, but liable to be somewhat marred if your next door neighbour may knock you off your box, stab you with a small pocket-knife, and jump on your stomach, all with grievous damage to you, but comparative immunity to himself. We are one day to have cheap law, meanwhile we have such cheap crime that injuries to the person are now within the reach of all. I may be a villain of the first water, if I have a few spare pounds in my pocket. From a careful survey of lately reported cases, I find I can run away with my neighbour's wife, seduce his daughter, half poison his household with adulterated food, and finally stab him with a pocket-knife, for rather less than £1000. Stabbing is so ridiculously cheap that I can indulge in it for a trifling penalty of £1. (See Southall's case.) But woe be to me if I dare to encroach on my neighbour's land, prejudice his trade, or touch his pocket ; then the law has remedies, vast and many, and I shall not only incur pecuniary penalties that are to all effects and purpose limitless, but I shall be made to suffer in person also. These two things are exactly indicative of the gradual decay of the national mind under the influence of two schools. The first teaches that man's primary object in life is to "get on in the world ; " hence we have this exaggerated estimate of the value and sanctity of property. The second school teaches that love can exist without reverence, mercy without justice, and liberty without obedience ; and as the logical result of such teaching, we have lost all clear and healthy knowledge of what justice really is, and invent a system of punishments which is not even really punitive, and without any element of retribution at all. Let us have instead a justice that not only condones the crime, but also makes a profit out of the criminal. And we get her; but note the irony of Fate: when our modern goddess *does* pluck up heart to be angry, she seems doomed to be angry in the wrong way, and with the wrong people. Here is a late instance (the printed report of which I send you) :—

William Hawkes, a blind man and very infirm, was brought up, having been committed from Marlborough Street, to be dealt with as a rogue and vagabond.

On being placed in the dock,

Mr. Montagu Williams, as *amicus curiæ*, said he had known the prisoner for years, from seeing him sitting on Waterloo Bridge tracing his fingers over a book designed for the blind to read, and in no instance had he seen him beg from those who passed by, so that he was practically doing no harm, and some time ago the late Sir William Bodkin had dealt very mercifully with him. Something ought to be done for him.

Mr. Harris said he could corroborate all that his learned friend had stated.

The Assistant-Judge said he had been convicted by the magistrate, and was sent here to be sentenced as a rogue and vagabond, *but the Court would not deal hardly with him*.

Horsford, chief officer of the Mendicity Society, said the prisoner had been frequently convicted for begging.

The Assistant-Judge sentenced him to be imprisoned for four months.—*May*, 1874.

The other day I was reading a beautiful Eastern story of a certain blind man who sat by the wayside begging; clearly a very importunate and troublesome blind man, who would by no means hold his peace, but who, nevertheless, had his heart's desire granted unto him at last. And yesterday I was also reading a very unlovely Western story of another blind man, who was "very infirm," not at all importunate, did not even beg, only sat there by the roadside and read out of a certain Book that has a great deal to say about justice and mercy. The sequel of the two stories varies considerably : in this latter one our civilized English Law clutches the old blind man by the throat, tells him he is a rogue and a vagabond, and flings him into prison for four months !

But our enlightened British Public is too busy clamouring for short deeds and cheap means of litigation, ever to give thought or time to mere "sentimental grievances." Have you seen the strange comment on Carlyle's letter of some months ago, in which he prophesied evil things to come, if England still persisted in doing her work "ill, swiftly, and mendaciously"? Our export trade, for the first five months of this year, shows a decrease of just eight millions ! The newspapers note with a horrified amazement, that the continental nations decline dealing any longer at the "old shop," and fall back on home products, and try to explain it by reference to the Capital and Labour question. Carlyle foresaw Germany's future, and told us plainly of it ; he foresees England's decadence, and warns us just as plainly of *that*, and the price we have already paid, in this year of grace 1874, for telling him to hold his tongue, is just eight millions.

Yours sincerely,

Next, or next but one, to the Fors for the squires, will come that for the lawyers. In the meantime, can any correspondent inform me, approximately, what the income and earnings of the legal profession are annually in England, and what sum is spent in collateral expenses for juries, witnesses, etc. ? The 'Times' for May 18th of this year gives the following estimate of the cost of the Tichborne trial, which seems to me very moderate —

THE TRIAL OF THE TICHBORNE CLAIMANT —On Saturday a return to the House of Commons, obtained by Mr. W. H. Smith, was printed, showing the amount expended upon the prosecution in the case of " Regina v Castro, otherwise Orton, otherwise Tichborne," and the probable amount still remaining to be paid out of the vote of Parliament for " this service " The probable cost of the trial is stated at £55,315 17*s*. 1*d*., of which £49,815 17*s*. 1*d* had been paid up to the 11th ult , and on the 11th of May inst. £5,500 remained unpaid. In 1872-3 counsels' fees were £1,146 16*s*. 6*d*., and in 1873-4 counsels' fees were £22,495 18*s* 4*d*. The jury were paid £3,780, and the shorthand writers £3,493 3*s*. The other expenses were witnesses, agents, etc., and law stationers and printing. Of the sum to be paid, £4,000 is for the Australian and Chili witnesses —*Times*, May 18th, 1874.

II. I reprint the following letter as it was originally published. I meant to have inquired into the facts a little farther, but have not had time.

21 MINCING LANE, LONDON, E C.
19th March, 1874.

Dear Sirs,—On the 27th March, 1872, we directed your attention to this subject of Usury in a paper headed " CHOOSE YOU THIS DAY WHOM YE WILL SERVE." We have since published our correspondence with the Rev Dr. Cumming, and we take his silence as an acknowledgment of his inability to justify his teaching upon this subject. We have also publicly protested against the apathy of the Bishops and Clergy of the Established Church regarding this national sin. We now append an extract from the ' Hampshire Independent' of the 11th instant, which has been forwarded to us —

" The Church of England in South Australia is in active competition with the money changers and those who sell doves The Church Office, Leigh Street, Adelaide, advertises that ' it is prepared to lend money at current rates—no commission or brokerage charged,' which is really liberal on the part of the Church of England, and may serve to distinguish it as a lender from the frequenters of the synagogues. It has been suggested that the Church Office should hang out the triple symbol of the Lombards, and that at the next examination of candidates for holy orders a few apposite questions might be asked, such as—'State concisely the best method of obtaining the highest rate of interest for Church moneys. Demonstrate how a system of Church money-lending was approved by the founder of Christianity.'"

As such perverseness can only end in sudden and over-whelming calamity, we make no apology for again urging you to assist us in our endeavours to banish the accursed element at least from our own trade.

Your obedient servants,

J. C. SILLAR AND CO.

I put in large print—it would be almost worth capital letters—the following statement of the principle of interest as "necessary to the existence of money." I suppose it is impossible to embody the modern view more distinctly —

"Money, the representation and measure of value, has also *the power to accumulate value by interest* (italics *not* mine). This accumulative power is essential to the existence of money, for no one will exchange productive property for money that does not represent production. The laws making gold and silver a public tender impart to dead masses of metal, as it were, life and animation.

---

* It is possible that this lending office may have been organised as a method of charity, corresponding to the original Monte di Pieta, the modern clergymen having imagined, in consequence of the common error about interest, that they could improve the system of Venice by ignoring its main condition—the lending gratis,—and benefit themselves at the same time.

They give them powers which without legal enactment they could not possess, and which enable their owner to obtain for their use what other men must earn by their labour. One piece of gold receives a legal capability to earn for its owner, in a given time, another piece of gold as large as itself; or in other words, the legal power of money to accumulate by interest compels the borrower in a given period, according to the rate of interest, to mine and coin, or to procure by the sale of his labour or products, another lump of gold as large as the first, and give it, together with the first, to the lender."—*Kellogg on Labour and Capital, New York,* 1849.

FORS CLAVIGERA.

LETTER THE 45th.

MY LORD DELAYETH HIS COMING
THE BRITISH SQUIRE

LUCCA, *2nd August*, 1874.

THE other day, in the Sacristan's cell at Assisi, I
got into a great argument with the Sacristan himself,
about the prophet Isaiah. It had struck me that I
should like to know what sort of a person his wife
was : and I asked my good host, over our morning's
coffee, whether the Church knew anything about her.
Brother Antonio, however, instantly and energetically
denied that he ever had a wife He was a 'Castissimo
profeta,'—how could I fancy anything so horrible of
him ! Vainly I insisted that, since he had children,
he must either have been married, or been under
special orders, like the prophet Hosea. But my Protestant Bible was good for nothing, said the Sacristan.
Nay, I answered, I never read, usually, in anything
later than a thirteenth century text ; let him produce
me one out of the convent library, and see if I
couldn't find Shearjashub in it. The discussion dropped

upon this,—because the library was inaccessible at the moment; and no printed Vulgate to be found. But I think of it again to-day, because I have just got into another puzzle about Isaiah,—to wit, what he means by calling himself a "man of unclean lips." * And that is a vital question, surely, to all persons venturing to rise up, as teachers ;—vital, at all events, to me, here, and now, for these following reasons.

Thirty years ago, I began my true study of Italian, and all other art,—here, beside the statue of Ilaria di Caretto, recumbent on her tomb. It turned me from the study of landscape to that of life, being then myself in the fullest strength of labour, and joy of hope.

And I was thinking, last night, that the drawing which I am now trying to make of it, in the weakness and despair of declining age, might possibly be the last I should make before quitting the study of Italian, and even all other, art, for ever.

I have no intent of doing so : quite the reverse of that. But I feel the separation between me and the people round me, so bitterly, in the world of my own which they cannot enter ; and I see their entrance to it now barred so absolutely by their own resolves, (they having deliberately and self-congratulatingly chosen for themselves the Manchester Cotton Mill instead of the Titian,) that it becomes every hour more urged upon

* Read Isaiah vi. through carefully.

me that I shall have to leave,—not father and mother, for they have left me; nor children, nor lands, for I have none,—but at least this spiritual land and fair domain of human art and natural peace,—because I am a man of unclean lips, and dwell in the midst of a people of unclean lips, and therefore am undone, because mine eyes have seen the King, the Lord of Hosts.

I say it, and boldly. Who else is there of you who can stand with me, and say the same? It is an age of progress, you tell me. Is your progress chiefly in this, that you *cannot* see the King, the Lord of Hosts, but only Baal, instead of Him?

"The Sun is God," said Turner, a few weeks before he died with the setting rays of it on his face.

He meant it, as Zoroaster meant it; and was a Sun-worshipper of the old breed. But the unheard-of foulness of your modern faith in Baal is its being faith *without* worship. The Sun is—*not* God,—you say. Not by any manner of means. A gigantic railroad accident, perhaps,—a coruscant δινος,—put on the throne of God like a limelight; and able to serve you, eventually, much better than ever God did.

I repeat my challenge. You,—Te-Deum-singing princes, colonels, bishops, choristers, and what else,— do any of you know what Te means? or what Deum? or what Laudamus? Have any of your eyes seen the King, or His Sabaoth? Will any of you say, with your hearts, 'Heaven and earth are full of His glory;

and in His name we will set up our banners, and do good work, whether we live or die ' ?

You, in especial, Squires of England, whose fathers were England's bravest and best,—by how much better and braver you are than your fathers, in this Age of Progress, I challenge you Have any of your eyes seen the King? Aie any of your hands ready for His work, and for His weapons,—even though they should chance to be pruning-hooks instead of spears ?

Who am I, that should challenge *you*—do you ask? My mother was a sailor's daughter, so please you ; one of my aunts was a baker's wife—the other, a tanner's , and I don't know much more about my family, except that there used to be a greengrocer of the name in a small shop near the Crystal Palace. Something of my early and vulgar life, if it interests you, I will tell in next Fors . in this one, it is indeed my business, poor gipsy herald as I am, to bring you such challenge, though you shall hunt and hang me for it.

Squires, are you, and not Workmen, nor Labourers, do you answer next ?

Yet, I have certainly sometimes seen engraved over your family vaults, and especially on the more modern tablets, those comfortful words, " Blessed are the dead which die in the Lord." But I observe that you are usually content, with the help of the village stone-mason, to say *only* this concerning your dead ; and that you but rarely venture to add the " yea " of the Spirit,

" that they may rest from their Labours, and their Works
do follow them." Nay, I am not even sure that many
of you clearly apprehend the meaning of such followers
and following ; nor, in the most pathetic funeral sermons,
have I heard the matter made strictly intelligible to
your hope. For indeed, though you have always
graciously considered your church no less essential a
part of your establishment than your stable, you have
only been solicitous that there should be no broken-
winded steeds in the one, without collateral endeavour
to find clerks for the other in whom the breath of the
Spirit should be unbroken also.

As yet it is a text which, seeing how often we
would fain take the comfort of it, surely invites
explanation. The implied difference between those who
die in the Lord, and die—otherwise ; the essential distinction between the labour from which these blessed
ones rest, and the work which in some mysterious way
follows them ; and the doubt—which must sometimes
surely occur painfully to a sick or bereaved squire—
whether the labours of his race are always severe
enough to make rest sweet, or the works of his race
always distinguished enough to make their following
superb,—ought, it seems to me, to cause the verse to glow
on your (lately, I observe, more artistic) tombstones,
like the letters on Belshazzar's wall ; and with the more
lurid and alarming light, that this " following " of the
works is distinctly connected, in the parallel passage of

Timothy, with " judgment " upon the works ; and that the kinds of them which can securely front such judgment, are there said to be, in some cases, " manifest beforehand," and, in no case, ultimately obscure.

" It seems to me," I say, as if such questions should occur to the squire during sickness, or funeral pomp. But the seeming is far from the fact. For I suppose the last idea which is likely ever to enter the mind of a representative squire, in any vivid or tenable manner, would be that anything he had ever done, or said, was liable to a judgment from superior powers ; or that any other law than his own will, or the fashion of his society, stronger than his will, existed in relation to the management of his estate. Whereas, according to any rational interpretation of our Church's doctrine, as by law established ; if there be one person in the world rather than another to whom it makes a serious difference whether he dies in the Lord or out of Him : and if there be one rather than another who will have strict scrutiny made into his use of every instant of his time, every syllable of his speech, and every action of his hand and foot,— on peril of having hand and foot bound, and tongue scorched, in Tophet,—that responsible person is the British Squire.

Very strange, the unconsciousness of this, in his own mind, and in the minds of all belonging to him. Even the greatest painter of him—the Reynolds who has filled England with the ghosts of her noble squires and dames,

—though he ends his last lecture in the Academy with " the *name* of Michael Angelo," never for an instant thought of following out the purposes of Michael Angelo, and painting a Last Judgment upon Squires, with the scene of it laid in Leicestershire. Appealing lords and ladies on either hand ;—" Behold, Lord, here is Thy land ; which I have—as far as my distressed circumstances would permit—laid up in a napkin. Perhaps there may be a cottage or so less upon it than when I came into the estate,—a tree cut down here and there imprudently ; —but the grouse and foxes are undiminished. Behold, there Thou hast that is Thine." And what capacities of dramatic effect in the cases of less prudent owners,— those who had said in their hearts, " My Lord delayeth His coming." Michael Angelo's St. Bartholomew, exhibiting his *own* skin flayed off him, awakes but a minor interest in that classic picture. How many an English squire might not we, with more pictorial advantage, see represented as adorned with the flayed skins of other people ? Micah the Morasthite, throned above them on the rocks of the mountain of the Lord, while his Master now takes up His parable, " Hear, I pray you, ye heads of Jacob, and ye princes of the house of Israel ; Is it not for you to know judgment, who also eat the flesh of my people, and flay their skin from off them, and they break their bones, and chop them in pieces as for the pot ? "

And how of the appeals on the other side ? " Lord,

Thou gavest me one land ; behold, I have gained beside it ten lands more." You think that an exceptionally economical landlord might indeed be able to say so much for himself; and that the increasing of their estates has at least been held a desirable thing by all of them, however Fortune, and the sweet thyme-scented Turf of England, might thwart their best intentions. Indeed it is well to have coveted—much more to have gained—increase of estate, in a certain manner. But neither the Morasthite nor his Master has any word of praise for you in appropriating surreptitiously, portions, say, of Hampstead Heath, or Hayes Common, or even any bit of gipsy-pot-boiling land at the roadside. Far the contrary : In that day of successful appropriation, there is one that shall take up a parable against you, and say, " We be utterly spoiled. He hath changed the portion of my people , turning away, he hath divided our fields. Therefore thou shalt have none that shall cast a cord by lot in the congregation of the Lord." In modern words, you shall have quite unexpected difficulties in getting your legal documents drawn up to your satisfaction ; and truly, as you have divided the fields of the poor, the poor, in their time, shall divide yours.

Nevertheless, in their deepest sense, those triumphant words, "Behold, I have gained beside it ten lands more," must be on the lips of every landlord who honourably enters into his rest ; whereas there will soon be considerable difficulty, as I think you are beginning to perceive, not only in gaining more, but even in keeping what you have got

For the gipsy hunt is up also, as well as Harry our King's ; and the hue and cry loud against your land and you ; your tenure of it is in dispute before a multiplying mob, deaf and blind as you,—frantic for the spoiling of you. The British Constitution is breaking fast. It never was, in its best days, entirely what its stout owner flattered himself. Neither British Constitution, nor British law, though it blanch every acre with an acre of parchment, sealed with as many seals as the meadow had buttercups, can keep your landlordships safe, henceforward, for an hour. You will have to fight for them as your fathers did, if you mean to keep them.

That is your only sound and divine right to them ; and of late you seem doubtful of appeal to it. You think political economy and peace societies will contrive some arithmetical evangel of possession. You will not find it so. If a man is not ready to fight for his land, and for his wife, no legal forms can secure them to him They can affirm his possession ; but neither grant, sanction, nor protect it. To his own love, to his own resolution, the lordship is granted ; and to those only.

That is the first ' labour ' of landlords, then. Fierce exercise of body and mind, in so much pugnacity as shall supersede all office of legal documents. Whatever labour you mean to put on your land, your first entirely Divine labour is to keep hold of it. And are you ready for that toil to-day ? It will soon be called for. Sooner or later, within the next few years, you will find yourselves in Parliament in front of a majority resolved on the establishment of a Republic, and the division of lands. Vainly the landed millowners will shriek for the " operation of natural laws of political economy." The vast natural law of carnivorous rapine which they have declared their Baal-God, in so many words, will be in *equitable* operation then , and not, as they fondly hoped to keep it, all on their own side. Vain, then, your arithmetical or sophistical defence. You may pathetically plead to the people's majority, that the divided lands will not give much more than the length and breadth of his grave to each mob-proprietor. They will answer, "We will have what we can get ;—at all events, *you* shall keep it no longer." And what will you do ? Send for the Life Guards and clear the House, and then, with all the respectable members of society as special constables, guard the streets ? That answered well against the Chartist meeting on Kennington Common in 1848. Yes; but in 1880 it will not be a Chartist meeting at Kennington, but a magna-and-maxima-Chartist Ecclesia at Westminster, that you must deal with. You will find a difference, and to purpose. Are you prepared to clear the streets with the Woolwich infant,—thinking that out of the mouth of that suckling, God would perfect your praise, and ordain your strength ? Be it so ; but every grocer's and chandler's shop in the thoroughfares of

London is a magazine of petroleum and percussion powder; and there are those who will use both, among the Republicans. And you will see your father the Devil's will done on earth, as it is in hell.

I call him your father, for you have denied your mortal fathers, and the Heavenly One. You have declared, in act and thought, the ways and laws of your sires—obsolete, and of your God—ridiculous , above all, the habits of obedience, and the elements of justice. You were made lords over God's heritage. You thought to make it your own heritage ; to be lords of your own land, not of God's land. And to this issue of ownership you are come.

And what a heritage it was, you *had* the lordship over ! A land of fruitful vales and pastoral mountains ; and a heaven of pleasant sunshine and kindly rain ; and times of sweet prolonged summer, and cheerful transient winter; and a race of pure heart, iron sinew, splendid fame, and constant faith.

All this was yours ! the earth with its fair fruits and innocent creatures ;—the firmament with its eternal lights and dutiful seasons ;—the men, souls and bodies, your fathers' true servants for a thousand years,—their lives, and their children's children's lives given into your hands, to save or to destroy ; their food yours,—as the grazing of the sheep is the shepherd's ; their thoughts yours,—priest and tutor chosen for them by you ; their hearts yours,—if you would but so much as know them by sight and name, and give them the passing grace of your own glance, as you dwelt among them, their king. And all this monarchy and glory, all this power and love, all this land and its people, you pitifullest, foulest of Iscariots, sopped to choking with the best of the feast from Christ's own fingers, you have deliberately sold to the highest bidder ;—Christ, and His Poor, and His Paradise together ; and instead of sinning only, like poor natural Adam, gathering of the fruit of the Tree of Knowledge, you, who don't want to gather it, *touch* it with a vengeance,—cut it down, and sell the timber.

Judases with the big bag—game-bag to wit !—to think how many of your dull Sunday mornings have been spent, for propriety's sake, looking chiefly at those carved angels blowing trumpets above your family vaults ; and never one of you has had Christianity enough in him to think that he might as easily have his moors full of angels as of grouse. And now, if ever you did see a real angel before the Day of Judgment, your first thought would be,—to shoot it.

And for your ' family ' vaults, what will be the use of them to you ? Does not Mr. Darwin show you that you can't wash the slugs out of a lettuce without disrespect to your ancestors ? Nay, the ancestors of the modern political economist cannot have been so pure ;—they were not—he tells you himself—vegetarian slugs, but carnivorous ones—those, to wit, that you see also carved on your tombstones, going in and out at the eyes of skulls. And truly, I don't know what else the holes in the heads of modern political economists were made for.

If there are any brighter windows in yours—if any audience chambers—if any council chambers—if any crown of walls that the pin of Death has not yet pierced,—it is time for you to rise to your work, whether you live or die.

What are you to do, then ? First,—the act which will be the foundation of all bettering and strength in your own lives, as in that of your tenants,—fix their rent ; under legal assurance that it shall not be raised , and under moral assurance that, if you see they treat your land well, and are likely to leave it to you, if they die, raised in value, the said rent shall be *diminished* in proportion to the improvement ; that is to say, providing they pay you the fixed rent during the time of lease, you are to leave to them the entire benefit of whatever increase they can give to the value of the land. Put the bargain in a simple instance. You lease them an orchard of crab-trees for so much a year ; they leave you at the end of the lease, an orchard of golden pippins. Supposing they have paid you their rent regularly, you have no right to anything more than what you lent them—crab-trees, to wit. You must pay them for the better trees which by their good industry they give you back, or, which is the same thing, previously reduce their rent in proportion to the improvement in apples. "The exact contrary," you observe, "of your present modes of proceeding." Just so, gentlemen ; and it is not improbable that the exact contrary in many other cases of your present modes of proceeding will be found by you, eventually, the proper one, and more than that, the necessary one. Then the second thing you have to do is to determine the income necessary for your own noble and peaceful country life ; and setting that aside out of the rents, for a constant sum, to be habitually lived well within limits of, put your heart and strength into the right employment of the rest for the bettering of your estates, in ways which the farmers for their own advantage could not or would not ; for the growth of more various plants ; the cherishing, not killing, of beautiful living creatures—bird, beast, and fish ; and the establishment of such schools of History, Natural History, and Art, as may enable your farmers' children, with your own, to know the meaning of the words Beauty, Courtesy, Compassion, Gladness, and Religion. Which last word, primarily, (you have not always forgotten to teach this one truth, because it chanced to suit your ends, and even the teaching of this one truth has been beneficent ;)—Religion, primarily, means ' Obedience '— binding to something, or some one. To be bound, or in bonds, as apprentice ; to be bound, or in bonds, by military oath ; to be bound, or in bonds, as a servant to man ; to be bound, or in bonds, under the yoke of God. These are all divinely instituted, eternally necessary, conditions of Religion ; beautiful, inviolable captivity and submission of soul in life and death. This essential meaning of Religion it was your office mainly to teach,—each of you captain and king, leader and lawgiver, to his people ;—vicegerents of your Captain, Christ. And now—you miserable jockeys and gamesters—you can't get a seat in Parliament for those all but worn-out buckskin breeches of yours, but by taking off your hats to the potboy. Pretty classical statues you will make, Coriolanuses of the nineteenth century, humbly promising, not to your people gifts of corn, but to your potboys, stealthy sale of adulterated beer !

· Obedience !—you dare not so much as utter the word, whether to potboy, or any other sort of boy, it seems, lately ; and the half of you still calling themselves Lords, Marquises, Sirs, and other such ancient names, which —though omniscient Mr. Buckle says they and their heraldry are nought—some little prestige lingers about still. You yourselves, what do you yet mean by them —Lords of what ?—Herrs, Signors, Dukes of what ?—of whom ? Do you mean merely, when you go to the root of the matter, that you sponge on the British farmer for your living, and are strong-bodied paupers compelling your dole ?

To that extent, there is still, it seems, some force in ·you. Heaven keep it in you ; for, as I have said, it will be tried, and soon ; and you would even yourselves see what was coming, but that in your hearts—not from cowardice, but from shame,—you are not sure whether you will be ready to fight for your dole ; and would fain persuade yourselves it will still be given you for form's sake, or pity's.

No, my lords and gentlemen,—you won it at the lance's point, and must so hold it, against the clubs of Sempach, if still you may. No otherwise. You won '*it*,' I say, —your dole,—as matters now stand. But perhaps, as matters used to stand, something else. As receivers of alms, you will find there is no fight in you. No beggar, nor herd of beggars, can fortify so very wide circumference of dish. And the real secret of those strange breakings of the lance by the clubs of Sempach, is—"that villanous saltpetre"—you think? No, Shakesperian lord ; nor even the sheaf-binding of Arnold, which so stopped the shaking of the fruitless spiculæ. The utter and inmost secret is, that you have been fighting these three hundred years for what you could *get* instead of what you could *give*. You were ravenous enough in rapine in the olden times ;* but you lived fearlessly and innocently by it, because, essentially, you wanted money and food to give,—not to consume ; to maintain your followers with, not to swallow yourselves. Your chivalry was founded, invariably, by knights who were content all their lives with their horse and armour and daily bread. Your kings, of true power, never desired for themselves more, down to the last of them, Friedrich. What they *did* desire was strength of man-

---

* The reader will perhaps now begin to see the true bearing of the earlier letters in Fors. Re-read, with this letter, that on the campaign of Crecy.

hood round them, and, in their own hands, the power of largesse.

'Largesse.' The French word is obsolete ; one Latin equivalent, Liberalitas, is fast receiving another, and not altogether similar significance, among English Liberals. The other Latin equivalent, Generosity, has become doubly meaningless, since modern political economy and politics neither require virtue, nor breeding. The Greek, or Greek-descended, equivalents—Charity, Grace, and the like, your Grace the Duke of —— can perhaps tell me what has become of *them.* Meantime, of all the words, 'Largesse,' the entirely obsolete one, is the perfectly chivalric one ; and therefore, next to the French description of Franchise, we will now read the French description of Largesse,—putting first, for comparison with it, a few more sentences * from the secretary's speech at the meeting of Social Science in Glasgow ; and remembering also the 'Pall Mall Gazette's' exposition of the perfection of Lord Derby's idea of agriculture, in the hands of the landowner—"Cultivating" (by machinery) "large farms *for himself.*"

" Exchange is the result, put into action, of the desire to possess that which belongs to another, controlled by reason and conscientiousness. It is difficult to conceive of any human transaction that cannot be resolved, in some form or other, into the idea of an

---

* I wish I could find room also for the short passages I omit ; but one I quoted before, " As no one will deny that man possesses carnivorous teeth," etc , and the others introduce collateral statements equally absurd, but with which at present we are not concerned.

exchange. All that *is* essential in production *are,"* (sic, only italics mine,) "directly evolved from this source."

* * * * *

" Man has therefore been defined to be an animal that exchanges. It will be seen, however, that he not only exchanges, but from the fact of his belonging, in part, to the order carnivora, that he also inherits, to a considerable degree, the desire to possess without exchanging; or, in other words, by fraud and violence, when such can be used for his own advantage, without danger to himself."

* * * * *

" Reason would immediately suggest to one of superior strength, that, however desirable it might be to take possession, by violence, of what another had laboured to produce, he might be treated in the same way by one stronger than himself; to which he, of course, would have great objection."

* * * * *

" In order, therefore, to prevent, or put a stop to, a practice which each would object to in his own case, and which, besides, would put a stop to production altogether, both reason and a sense of justice would suggest the act of exchange, as the only proper mode of obtaining things from one another."

* * * * *

To anybody who *had* either reason or a sense of justice, it might possibly have suggested itself that, except for the novelty of the thing, *mere* exchange profits nobody, and presupposes a coincidence, or rather a harmonious dissent, of opinion not always attainable.

Mr. K. has a kettle, and Mr. P. has a pot. Mr. P. says to Mr. K., 'I would rather have your kettle than my pot;' and if, coincidently, Mr. K. is also in a discontented humour, and can say to Mr. P., 'I would rather have your pot than my kettle,' why—both Hanses are in luck, and all is well . but is their carnivorous instinct thus to be satisfied ? Carnivorous instinct says, in both cases, ' I want both pot and kettle myself, and you to have neither,' and is entirely unsatisfiable on the principle of exchange. The ineffable blockhead who wrote the paper forgot that the principle of division of labour *underlies* that of exchange, and does not arise out of it, but is the only reason for it. If Mr. P. can make two pots, and Mr. K. two kettles, and so, by exchange, both become possessed of a pot and a kettle, all is well. But the profit of the business is in the additional production, and only the convenience in the subsequent exchange. For, indeed, there are in the main two great fallacies which the rascals of the world rejoice in making its fools proclaim : the first, that by continually exchanging, and cheating each other on exchange, two exchanging persons, out of one pot, alternating with one kettle, can make their two fortunes. That is the principle of *Trade.* The second, that Judas' bag has become a juggler's, in which, if Mr. P. deposits his pot, and waits awhile, there will come out two pots, both full of broth ; and Mr. K deposits his kettle, and waits awhile, there will come out two kettles both full of fish ! That is the principle of *Interest.*

However, for the present, observe simply the conclusion of our social science expositor, that "the art of exchange is the only proper mode of obtaining things from one another ; " and now compare with this theory that of old chivalry, namely, that gift was also a good way, both of losing and gaining.

> " And after, in the dance, went
>   Largesse, that set all her intent
>   For to be honourable and free.
>   Of Alexander's kin was she ;
>   Her mosté joy was, I wis,
>   When that she gave, and said, ' Have this.'*
>   Not Avarice, the foul caitiff,†
>   Was half, to gripe, so ententive,
>   As Largesse is to give, and spend.
>   And God always enough her send, (sent)
>   So that the more she gave away,
>   The more, I wis, she had alway.

*   *   *   *

* I must warn you against the false reading of the original, in many editions. Fournier's five volume one is altogether a later text, in some cases with interesting intentional modifications, probably of the fifteenth century ; but oftener with destruction of the older meaning It gives this couplet, for instance,—

> " Si n'avoit el plaisir de rien,
>   Que quant elle donnoit du sien."

The old reading is,

> " Si n'avoit elle joie de rien,
>   Fors quant elle povoit dire, 'tien.'

Didot's edition, Paris, 1814, is founded on very early and valuable texts ; but it is difficult to read. Chaucer has translated a text some twenty or thirty years later in style ; and his English is quite trustworthy as far as it is carried. For the rest of the Romance, Fournier's text is practically good enough, and easily readable.

† Fr. 'chetive,' rhyming accurately to 'ententive.'

Largesse had on a robe fresh
Of rich purpure, sarlinish ; *
Well formed was her face, and clear,
And open had she her colere, (collar)
For she right then had in present
Unto a lady made present
Of a gold brooch, full well wrought ;
And certes, it mis-set her nought,
For through her smocke, wrought with silk,
The flesh was seen as white as milke."

Think over that, ladies, and gentlemen who love them, for a pretty way of being decolletée. Even though the flesh should be a little sunburnt sometimes,—so that it be the Sun of Righteousness, and not Baal, who shines on it—though it darken from the milk-like flesh to the colour of the Madonna of Chartres,—in this world you shall be able to say, I am black, but comely ; and, dying, shine as the brightness of the firmament—as the stars for ever and ever. *They* do not receive their glories,—however one differeth in glory from another,—either by, or on, Exchange.

LUCCA. (*Assumption of the Virgin.*)

'As the stars, *for ever.*' Perhaps we had better not say that,—modern science looking pleasantly forward to the extinction of a good many of them. But it

* Fr. Sarrasinesse.

will be well to shine like them, if but for a little while

You probably did not understand why, in a former letter, the Squire's special duty towards the peasant was said to be " presenting a celestial appearance to him."

That is, indeed, his appointed missionary work ; and still more definitely, his wife's.

The giving of loaves is indeed the lady's first duty ; the first, but the least.

Next, comes the giving of brooches ;—seeing that her people are dressed charmingly and neatly, as well as herself, and have pretty furniture, like herself.*

But her chief duty of all—is to be, Herself, lovely.

> " That through her smocke, wrought with silk,
>   The flesh be seen as white as milke." †

Flesh, ladies mine, you observe ; and not any merely illuminated resemblance of it, after the fashion of the daughter of Ethbaal.   It is your duty to be

---

* Even after eighteen hundred years of sermons, the Christian public do not clearly understand that 'two coats,' in the brief sermon of the Baptist to repentance, mean also, two petticoats, and the like

I am glad that Fors obliges me to finish this letter at Lucca, under the special protection of St. Martin.

† Fr.,   ' Si que par oula la chemise
                  Lui blancheoit la char alise "

Look out 'Alice,' in Miss Yonge's Dictionary of Christian Names, and remember Alice of Salisbury.

lovely, not by candlelight, but sunshine; not out of a window or opera-box, but on the bare ground

Which that you may be,—if through the smocke the flesh, then, much more, through the flesh, the spirit must be seen "as white as milke."

I have just been drawing, or trying to draw, Giotto's 'Poverty' (Sancta Paupertas) at Assisi. You may very likely know the chief symbolism of the picture: that Poverty is being married to St. Francis, and that Christ marries them, while her bare feet are entangled in thorns, but behind her head is a thicket of rose and lily. It is less likely you should be acquainted with the farther details of the group

The thorns are of the acacia, which, according to tradition, was used to weave Christ's crown. The roses are in two clusters,—palest red,* and deep crimson; the one on her right, the other on her left, above her head, pure white on the golden ground, rise the Annunciation Lilies. She is not crowned with them, observe; they are behind her: she is crowned only with her own hair, wreathed in a tress with which she had bound her short bridal veil. For dress, she has—her smocke only; and *that* torn, and torn again, and patched, diligently, except just at the shoulders, and a little below the throat, where Giotto

---

* I believe the pale roses are meant to be white, but are tinged with red that they may not contend with the symbolic brightness of the lilies

has torn it, too late for her to mend ; and the fair flesh is seen through, so white that one cannot tell where the rents are, except when quite close.

For girdle, she has the Franciscan's cord ; but that also is white, as if spun of silk ; her whole figure, like a statue of snow, seen against the shade of her purple wings : for she is already one of the angels.   A crowd of them, on each side, attend her ; two, her sisters, are her bridesmaids also.   Giotto has written their names above them—SPES , KARITAS ;—their sister's Christian name he has written in the lilies, for those of us who have truly learned to read.   Charity is *crowned* with white roses, which burst, as they open, into flames ; and she gives the bride a marriage gift

" An apple," say the interpreters.

Not so.   It was some one else than Charity who gave the first bride *that* gift.   It is a heart.

Hope only points upwards ; and while Charity has the golden nimbus round her head circular (infinite), like that of Christ and the eternal angels, *she* has her glory set within the lines that limit the cell of the bee,—hexagonal.

And the bride has hers, also, so restricted : nor though she and her bridesmaids are sisters, are they dressed alike ; but one in red ; and one in green ; and one, robe, flesh and spirit, a statue of Snow,

"La terza parea neve, teste mossa."

Do you know now, any of you, ladies mine, what Giotto's lilies mean between the roses? or how they may also grow among the Sesame of knightly spears?

Not one of you, maid or mother, though I have besought you these four years, (except only one or two of my personal friends,) has joined St. George's Company. You probably think St. George may advise some different arrangements in Hanover Square? It is possible; for his own knight's cloak is white, and he may wish you to bear such celestial appearance constantly. You talk often of bearing Christ's cross, do you never think of putting on Christ's robes,—those that He wore on Tabor? nor know what lamps they were which the wise virgins trimmed for the marriage feast? You think, perhaps, you can go in to that feast in gowns made half of silk, and half of cotton, spun in your Lancashire cotton-mills; and that the Americans have struck oil enough—(lately, I observe also, native gas,) —to supply any number of belated virgins?

It is not by any means so, fair ladies. It is only your newly adopted Father who tells you so. Suppose, learning what it is to be generous, you recover your descent from God, and then weave your household dresses white with your own fingers? For as no fuller on earth can white them, but the light of a living faith,—so no demon under the earth can darken them like the shadow of a dead one. And your modern English 'faith without works' *is* dead; and would to God she were buried too, for the stench of her goes up to His throne from a thousand fields of blood. *Weave,* I say,—you have trusted far too much lately to the washing,—your household raiment white ; go out in the morning to Ruth's field, to sow as well as to glean ; sing your Te Deum, at evening, thankfully, as God's daughters,—and there shall be no night there, for your light shall so shine before men that they may see your good works, and glorify—not Baal the railroad accident—but

"L'Amor che muove il Sole, e l'altre stelle."

NOTES AND CORRESPONDENCE.

———◆———

I have had by me for some time a small pamphlet, "The Agricultural Labourer, by a Farmer's Son," kindly sent me by the author. The matter of it is excellent as far as it reaches; but the writer speaks as if the existing arrangements between landlord, farmer, and labourer must last for ever. If he will look at the article on "Peasant Farming" in the 'Spectator' of July 4th of this year, he may see grounds for a better hope. That article is a review of Mr. W. Thornton's "Plea for Peasant Proprietors," and the following paragraph from it may interest, and perhaps surprise, other readers besides my correspondent. Its first sentence considerably surprises *me*, to begin with; so I have italicized it :—

" *This country is only just beginning to be seriously roused to the fact that it has an agricultural question at all,* and some of those most directly interested therein are, in their pain and surprise at the discovery, hurrying so fast the wrong way, that it will probably take a long time to bring them round again to sensible thoughts, after most of the rest of the community are ready with an answer.

"The primary object of this book is to combat the pernicious error of a large school of English economists with reference to the hurtful character of small farms and small landed properties. . . . One would think that the evidence daily before a rural economist, in the marvellous extra production of a market garden, or even a peasant's allotment, over an ordinary farm, might suffice to raise doubts whether

* Macintosh, 24, Paternoster Row

vast fields tilled by steam, weeded by patent grubbers, and left otherwise to produce in rather a happy-go-lucky fashion, were likely to be the most advanced and profitable of all cultivated lands. On this single point of production, Mr. Thornton conclusively proves the small farmer to have the advantage.

"The extreme yields of the very highest English farming are even exceeded in Guernsey, and in that respect the evidence of the greater productiveness of small farming over large is overwhelming. The Channel Islands not only feed their own population, but are large exporters of provisions as well.

"Small farms being thus found to be more advantageous, it is but an easy step to peasant proprietors."

Stop a moment, Mr. Spectator. The step is easy, indeed, —so is a step into a well, or out of a window. There is no question whatever, in any country, or at any time, respecting the expediency of small farming; but whether the small farmer should be the proprietor of his land, *is* a very awkward question indeed in some countries. Are you aware, Mr. Spectator, that your 'easy step,' taken in two lines and a breath, means what I, with all my Utopian zeal, have been fourteen years writing on Political Economy, without venturing to hint at, except under my breath,—some considerable modification, namely, in the position of the existing · British landlord ?—nothing less, indeed, if your 'step' were to be completely taken, than the reduction of him to a 'small peasant proprietor'? And unless he can show some reason against it, the 'easy step' will most assuredly be taken with him.

Yet I have assumed, in this Fors, that it is not to be taken. That under certain modifications of his system of Rent, he may still remain lord of his land,—may, and ought, provided always he knows what it is to be lord of *any*thing. Of which I hope to reason farther in the Fors for November of this year.

FORS CLAVIGERA.

LETTER THE 46th.

THE SACRISTAN

FLORENCE, 28th August, 1874

I INTENDED this letter to have been published on my
mother's birthday, the second of next month. Fors,
however, has entirely declared herself against that arrangement, having given me a most unexpected piece of
work here, in drawing the Emperor, King, and Baron,
who, throned by Simone Memmi beneath the Duomo
of Florence, beside a Pope, Cardinal, and Bishop, represented, to the Florentine mind of the fourteenth century,
the sacred powers of the State in their fixed relation
to those of the Church. The Pope lifts his right
hand to bless, and holds the crosier in his left , having
no powers but of benediction and protection. The
Emperor holds his sword upright in his right hand,
and a skull in his left, having alone the power of
death. Both have triple crowns , but the Emperor
alone has a nimbus. The King has the diadem of
fleur-de-lys, and the ball and globe , the Cardinal, a

book. The Baron has his warrior's sword; the Bishop,
a pastoral staff. And the whole scene is very beautifully expressive of what have been by learned authors
supposed the Republican or Liberal opinions of Florence,
in her day of pride.

The picture (fresco), in which this scene occurs, is
the most complete piece of theological and political
teaching given to us by the elder arts of Italy; and
this particular portion of it is of especial interest to
me, not only as exponent of the truly liberal and com-
munist principles which I am endeavouring to enforce
in these letters for the future laws of the St. George's
Company; but also because my maternal grandmother
was the landlady of the Old King's Head in Market
Street, Croydon; and I wish she were alive again, and
I could paint her Simone Memmi's King's head, for a
sign.

My maternal grandfather was, as I have said, a
sailor, who used to embark, like Robinson Crusoe, at
Yarmouth, and come back at rare intervals, making
himself very delightful at home. I have an idea he
had something to do with the herring business, but
am not clear on that point; my mother never being
much communicative concerning it. He spoiled her,
and her (younger) sister, with all his heart, when he
was at home; unless there appeared any tendency to
equivocation, or imaginative statements, on the part of
the children, which were always unforgiveable. My

mother being once perceived by him to have distinctly told him a lie, he sent the servant out forthwith to buy an entire bundle of new broom twigs to whip her with. "They did not hurt me so much as one would have done," said my mother, "but I *thought* a good deal of it."

My grandfather was killed at two-and-thirty, by trying to ride, instead of walk, into Croydon; he got his leg crushed by his horse against a wall; and died of the hurt's mortifying. My mother was then seven or eight years old, and, with her sister, was sent to quite a fashionable (for Croydon) day-school, (Mrs. Rice's,) where my mother was taught evangelical principles, and became the pattern girl and best sewer in the school; and where my aunt absolutely refused evangelical principles, and became the plague and pet of it.

My mother, being a girl of great power, with not a little pride, grew more and more exemplary in her entirely conscientious career, much laughed at, though much beloved, by her sister, who had more wit, less pride, and no conscience. At last my mother, being a consummate housewife, was sent for to Scotland to take care of my paternal grandfather's house; who was gradually ruining himself; and who at last effectually ruined, and killed, himself My father came up to London; was a clerk in a merchant's house for nine years, without a holiday; then began business on his own account ; paid his father's debts ; and married his exemplary Croydon cousin.

Meantime my aunt had remained in Croydon, and married a baker. By the time I was four years old, and beginning to recollect things,—my father rapidly taking higher commercial position in London,—there was traceable—though to me, as a child, wholly incomprehensible —just the least possible shade of shyness on the part of Hunter Street, Brunswick Square, towards Market Street, Croydon. But whenever my father was ill,—and hard work and sorrow had already set their mark on him, —we all went down to Croydon to be petted by my homely aunt ; and walk on Duppas Hill, and on the heather of Addington

(And now I go on with the piece of this letter written last month at Assisi.)

My aunt lived in the little house still standing—or which was so four months ago—the fashionablest in Market Street, having actually two windows over the shop, in the second story ; but I never troubled myself about that superior part of the mansion, unless my father happened to be making drawings in Indian ink, when I would sit reverently by and watch ; my chosen domains being, at all other times, the shop, the bakehouse, and the stones round the spring of crystal water at the back door (long since let down into the modern sewer) ; and my chief companion, my aunt's dog, Towzer, whom she had taken pity on when he was a snappish starved vagrant, and made a brave and affectionate dog of, which was the kind of thing she did for every living creature that came in her way, all her life long.

I am sitting now in the Sacristan's cell at Assisi. Its roof is supported by three massive beams,—not squared beams, but tree trunks barked, with the grand knots left in them, answering all the purpose of sculpture. The walls are of rude white plaster, though there is a Crucifixion by Giottino on the back of one, outside the door; the floor, brick; the table, olive wood; the windows two, and only about four feet by two in the opening, (but giving plenty of light in the sunny morning, aided by the white walls,) looking out on the valley of the Tescio. Under one of them, a small arched stove for cooking; in a square niche beside the other, an iron wash-hand stand,—that is to say, a tripod of good fourteenth century work, carrying a grand brown porringer, two feet across, and half a foot deep. Between the windows is the fireplace, the wall above it rich brown with the smoke. Hung against the wall behind me are a saucepan, gridiron, and toasting-fork; and in the wall a little door, closed only by a brown canvas curtain, opening to an inner cell nearly filled by the bedstead, and at the side of the room a dresser, with cupboard below, and two wine flasks, and three pots of Raphael ware on the top of it, together with the first volume of the 'Maraviglie di Dio nell' anime del Purgatorio, del padre Carlo Gregorio Rosignoli, della Compagnia de Gesu,' (Roma, 1841). There is a bird singing outside, a constant low hum of flies, making the ear sure it is summer; a dove cooing, very low; and absolutely nothing else to be heard, I find, after listening with great care. And I feel entirely at home, because the room—except in the one point of being extremely dirty—is just the kind of thing I used to see in my aunt's bakehouse, and the country and the sweet valley outside still rest in peace, such as used to be on the Surrey hills in the olden days.

And now I am really going to begin my steady explanation of what the St George's Company have to do

1. You are to do good work, whether you live or die. 'What *is* good work?' you ask. Well you may! For your wise pastors and teachers, though they have been very careful to assure you that good works are the fruits of faith, and follow after justification, have been so certain of that fact that they never have been the least solicitous to explain to you, and still less to discover for themselves, what good works *were,* content if they perceived a general impression on the minds of their congregations that good works meant going to church and admiring the sermon on Sundays, and making as much money as possible in the rest of the week.

It is true, one used to hear almsgiving and prayer sometimes recommended by old-fashioned country ministers. But "the poor are now to be raised without gifts," says my very hard-and-well-working friend Miss Octavia Hill ; and prayer is entirely inconsistent with the laws of hydro (and other) statics, says the Duke of Argyll.

It may be so, for aught I care, just now. Largesse and supplication may or may not be still necessary in the world's economy. They are not, and never were, part of the world's work. For no man can give till he has been paid his own wages ; and still less can he ask his Father for the said wages till he has done his day's duty for them.

Neither almsgiving nor praying, therefore, nor psalm-singing, nor even—as poor Livingstone thought, to his own death, and our bitter loss—discovering the mountains of the Moon, have anything to do with "good work," or God's work. But it is not so very difficult to discover what that work is You keep the Sabbath, in imitation of God's rest. Do, by all manner of means, if you like ; and keep also the rest of the week in imitation of God's work.

It is true that, according to tradition, that work was done a long time ago, "before the chimneys in Zion were hot, and ere the present years were sought out, and or ever the inventions of them that now sin, were turned , and before they were sealed that have gathered faith for a treasure."* But the established processes of

* 2 Esdras vi 4, 5

it continue, as his Grace of Argyll has argutely observed ;—and your own work will be good, if it is in harmony with them, and duly sequent of them. Nor are even the first main facts or operations by any means inimitable, on a duly subordinate scale, for if Man be made in God's image, much more is Man's work made to be the image of God's work. So therefore look to your model, very simply stated for you in the nursery tale of Genesis.

Day First.—The Making, or letting in, of Light.

Day Second.—The Discipline and Firmament of Waters.

Day Third—The Separation of earth from water, and planting the secure earth with trees.

Day Fourth—The Establishment of time and seasons, and of the authority of the stars.

Day Fifth—Filling the water and air with fish and birds.

Day Sixth—Filling the land with beasts ; and putting divine life into the clay of one of these, that it may have authority over the others, and over the rest of the Creation.

Here is your nursery story,—very brief, and in some sort unsatisfactory ; not altogether intelligible, (I don't know anything very good that is,) nor wholly indisputable, (I don't know anything ever spoken usefully on so wide a subject that is); but substantially vital and sufficient. So the good human work may properly divide itself into the same six branches; and will be a perfectly literal and practical following out of the Divine; and will have opposed to it a correspondent Diabolic force of eternally bad work—as much worse than idleness or death, as good work is better than idleness or death.

Good work, then, will be,—

A. Letting in light where there was darkness; as especially into poor rooms and back streets; and generally guiding and administering the sunshine wherever we can, by all the means in our power.

And the correspondent Diabolic work is putting a tax on windows, and blocking out the sun's light with smoke.

B. Disciplining the falling waters. In the Divine work, this is the ordinance of clouds;* in the human it is properly putting the clouds to service; and first stopping the rain where they carry it from the sea, and then keeping it pure as it goes back to the sea again.

And the correspondent Diabolic work is the arrangement of land so as to throw all the water back to the sea as fast as we can;† and putting every sort of filth into the stream as it runs.

---

* See 'Modern Painters,' vol. III, ' The Firmament."
† Compare Dante, Purg , end of Canto V.

c. The separation of earth from water, and planting it with trees. The correspondent human work is especially clearing morasses, and planting desert ground.

The Dutch, in a small way, in their own country, have done a good deal with sand and tulips; also the North Germans. But the most beautiful type of the literal ordinance of dry land in water is the State of Venice, with her sea-canals, restrained, traversed by their bridges, and especially bridges of the Rivo Alto or High Bank, which are, or were till a few years since, symbols of the work of a true Pontifex,—the Pontine Marshes being the opposite symbol.

The correspondent Diabolic work is turning good land and water into mud; and cutting down trees that we may drive steam ploughs, etc., etc.

d. The establishment of times and seasons. The correspondent human work is a due watching of the rise and set of stars, and course of the sun; and due administration and forethought of our own annual labours, preparing for them in hope, and concluding them in joyfulness, according to the laws and gifts of Heaven. Which beautiful order is set forth in symbols on all lordly human buildings round the semicircular arches which are types of the rise and fall of days and years.

And the correspondent Diabolic work is turning night into day with candles, so that we never see the stars; and mixing the seasons up one with another, and having early strawberries, and green pease and the like.

E. Filling the waters with fish, and air with birds. The correspondent human work is Mr Frank Buckland's and the like,—of which 'like' I am thankful to have been permitted to do a small piece near Croydon, in the streams to which my mother took me when a child, to play beside. There were more than a dozen of the fattest, shiniest, spottiest, and tamest trout I ever saw in my life, in the pond at Carshalton, the last time I saw it this spring.

The correspondent Diabolic work is poisoning fish, as is done at Coniston, with copper-mining ; and catching them for ministerial and other fashionable dinners when they ought not to be caught ; and treating birds—as birds are treated, Ministerially and otherwise.

F. Filling the earth with beasts, properly known and cared for by their master, Man ; but chiefly breathing into the clayey and brutal nature of Man himself, the Soul, or Love, of God.

The correspondent Diabolic work is shooting and tormenting beasts ; and grinding out the soul of man from his flesh, with machine labour ; and then grinding down the flesh of him, when nothing else is left, into clay, with machines for that purpose—mitrailleuses, Woolwich infants, and the like.

These are the six main heads of God's and the Devil's work.

And as Wisdom, or Prudentia, is with God, and with
His children in the doing,—"There I was by Him, as
one brought up with Him, and I was daily His delight,"
—so Folly, or Stultitia, saying, There is no God, is with
the Devil and his children, in the *un*doing. " There she
is with them as one brought up with them, and she is
daily their delight."

And so comes the great reverse of Creation, and wrath
of God, accomplished on the earth by the fiends, and
by men their ministers, seen by Jeremy the Prophet :
" For my people is foolish, they have not known me ,
they are sottish children, and they have none understanding : they are wise to do evil, but to do good they
have no knowledge.   [Now note the reversed creation.]
I beheld the Earth, and, lo, it was without form, and
void ; and the Heavens, and they had no light.   I
beheld the mountains, and, lo, they trembled, and all
the hills moved lightly.   I beheld, and, lo, there was
no man, and all the birds of the heavens were fled.   I
beheld, and, lo, the fruitful place was a wilderness, and
all the cities thereof were broken down at the presence
of the Lord, and by His fierce anger."

And so, finally, as the joy and honour of the ancient
and divine Man and Woman were in their children, so
the grief and dishonour of the modern and diabolic
Man and Woman are in their children ; and as the
Rachel of Bethlehem weeps for her children, and will
not be comforted, because they are not, the Rachel of

England weeps for her children, and will not be comforted—because they are.

Now, whoever you may be, and how little your power may be, and whatever sort of creature you may be,—man, woman, or child,—you can, according to what discretion of years you may have reached, do something of this Divine work, or *undo* something of this Devil's work, every day. Even if you are a slave, forced to labour at some abominable and murderous trade for bread,—as iron-forging, for instance, or gunpowder-making,—you can resolve to deliver yourself, and your children after you, from the chains of that hell, and from the dominion of its slave-masters, or to die. That is Patriotism, and true desire of Freedom, or Franchise. What Egyptian bondage, do you suppose—(painted by Mr Poynter as if it 'were a thing of the past !)—was ever so cruel as a modern English iron forge, with its steam hammers ? What Egyptian worship of garlic or crocodile ever so damnable as modern English worship of money ? Israel—even by the fleshpots—was sorry to have to cast out her children,—would fain stealthily keep her little Moses,—if Nile were propitious, and roasted her passover anxiously. But English Mr. P., satisfied with his fleshpot, and the broth of it, will not be over-hasty about his roast. If the Angel, perchance, should *not* pass by, it would be no such matter, thinks Mr. P.

Or, again, if you are a slave to Society, and must do

what the people next door bid you,—you can resolve, with any vestige of human energy left in you, that you will indeed put a few things into God's fashion, instead of the fashion of next door. Merely fix that on your mind as a thing to be done ; to have things—dress, for instance,—according to God's taste, (and I can tell you He is likely to have some, as good as any modiste you know of) ; or dinner, according to God's taste instead of the Russians' ; or supper, or picnic, with guests of God's inviting, occasionally, mixed among the more respectable company.

By the way, I wrote a letter to one of my lady friends, who gives rather frequent dinners, the other day, which may perhaps be useful to others . it was to this effect mainly, though I add and alter a little to make it more general —

" You probably will be having a dinner-party to-day ; now, please do this, and remember I am quite serious in what I ask you. We all of us, who have any belief in Christianity at all, wish that Christ were alive now. Suppose, then, that He is. I think it very likely that if He were in London, you would be one of the people whom He would take some notice of. Now, suppose He has sent you word that He is coming to dine with you to-day ; but that you are not to make any change in your guests on His account ; that He wants to meet exactly the party you have ; and no other. Suppose you have just received this message, and that St. John has

also left word, in passing, with the butler, that his
Master will come alone; so that you won't have any
trouble with the Apostles. Now this is what I want
you to do. First, determine what you will have for
dinner. You are not ordered, observe, to make no
changes in your bill of fare. Take a piece of paper,
and absolutely *write* fresh orders to your cook,—you
can't realise the thing enough without writing. That
done, consider how you will arrange your guests—who
is to sit next Christ on the other side—who opposite,
and so on; finally, consider a little what you will talk
about, supposing, which is just possible, that Christ
should tell you to go on talking as if He were not
there, and never to mind *Him* You couldn't, you will
tell me? Then, my dear lady, how can you in general?
Don't you profess—nay, don't you much more than
profess—to believe that Christ *is* always there, whether
you see Him or not? Why should the seeing make
such a difference?"

But you are no master or mistress of household?
You are only a boy, or a girl What can you do?

We will take the work of the third day, for its
range is at once lower and wider than that of the
others. Can you do *nothing* in that kind? Is there
no garden near you where you can get from some
generous person leave to weed the beds, or sweep
up the dead leaves? (I once allowed an eager little girl
of ten years old to weed my garden; and now, though

it is long ago, she always speaks as if the favour had
been done to *her*, and not to the garden and me.)
Is there no dusty place that you can water ?—if it be
only the road before your door, the traveller will thank
you. No roadside ditch that you can clean of its clogged
rubbish, to let the water run clear ? No scattered heap
of brickbats that you can make an ordinary pile of ?
You are ashamed ? Yes ; that false shame is the Devil's
pet weapon. He does more work with it even than
with false pride. For with false pride, he only goads
evil ; but with false shame, paralyzes good.

But you have no ground of your own, you are a
girl, and can't work on other people's ? At least you
have a window of your own, or one in which you have
a part interest. With very little help from the carpenter, you can arrange a safe box outside of it, that
will hold earth enough to root something in. If you
have any favour from Fortune at all, you can train a
rose, or a honeysuckle, or a convolvulus, or a nasturtium,
round your window—a quiet branch of ivy—or if for
the sake of its leaves only, a tendril or two of vine.
Only, be sure all your plant-pots are kept well outside
of the window. Don't come to having pots in the room,
unless you are sick.

I got a nice letter from a young girl, not long since,
asking why I had said in my answers to former questions that young ladies were " to have nothing to do
with greenhouses, still less with hothouses." The new

inquirer has been sent me by Fors, just when it was time to explain what I meant.

First, then—The primal object of your gardening, for yourself, is to keep you at work in the open air, whenever it is possible. The greenhouse will always be a refuge to you from the wind , which, on the contrary, you ought to be able to bear ; and will tempt you into clippings and pottings and pettings, and mere standing dilettantism in a damp and over-scented room, instead of true labour in fresh air.

Secondly.—It will not only itself involve unnecessary expense—(for the greenhouse is sure to turn into a hothouse in the end , and even if not, is always having its panes broken, or its blinds going wrong, or its stands getting rickety) , but it will tempt you into buying nursery plants, and waste your time in anxiety about them.

Thirdly.—The use of your garden to the household ought to be mainly in the vegetables you can raise in it. And, for these, your proper observance of season, and of the authority of the stars, is a vital duty. Every climate gives its vegetable food to its living creatures at the right time ; your business is to know that time, and be prepared for it, and to take the healthy luxury which nature appoints you, in the rare annual taste of the thing given in those its due days. The vile and gluttonous modern habit of forcing never allows people properly to taste anything.

Lastly, and chiefly.—Your garden is to enable you to obtain such knowledge of plants as you may best use in the country in which you live by communicating it to others; and teaching them to take pleasure in the green herb, given for meat, and the coloured flower, given for joy. And your business is not to make the greenhouse or hothouse rejoice and blossom like the rose, but the wilderness and solitary place. And it is, therefore, (look back to Letter 26th, p. 15,) not at all of camellias and air-plants that the devil is afraid; on the contrary, the Dame aux Camellias is a very especial servant of his, and the Fly-God of Ekron himself superintends—as you may gather from Mr. Darwin's recent investigations—the birth and parentage of the orchidaceæ. But he is mortally afraid of roses and crocuses.

Of roses, that is to say, growing wild;—(what lovely hedges of them there were, in the lane leading from Dulwich College up to Windmill (or Gipsy) Hill, in my aunt's time!)—but of the massy horticultural-prize rose, —fifty pounds' weight of it on a propped bush—he stands in no awe whatever; not even when they are cut afterwards and made familiar to the poor in the form of bouquets, so that poor Peggy may hawk them from street to street—and hate the smell of them, as his own imps do. For Mephistopheles knows there are poorer Margarets yet than Peggy.

Hear *this*, you fine ladies of the houses of York and

Lancaster, and you, new-gilded Miss Kilmanseggs, with your gardens of Gul,—you, also, evangelical expounders of the beauty of the Rose of Sharon,—it is a bit of a letter just come to me from a girl of good position in the manufacturing districts :—

"The other day I was coming through a nasty part of the road, carrying a big bunch of flowers, and met two dirty, ragged girls, who looked eagerly at my flowers Then one of them said, 'Give us a flower!' I hesitated, for she looked and spoke rudely, but when she ran after me, I stopped; and pulled out a large rose, and asked the other girl which she would like. 'A red one, the same as hers,' she answered. They actually did not know its name Poor girls! they promised to take care of them, and went away looking rather softened and pleased, I thought, but perhaps they would pull them to pieces, and laugh at the success of their boldness. At all events, they made me very sad and thoughtful for the rest of my walk."

And, I hope, a little so, even when you got home again, young lady. Meantime, are you quite sure of your fact; and that there was no white rose in your bouquet, from which the " red one" might be distinguished, without naming ? In any case, my readers have enough to think of, for this time, I believe

NOTES AND CORRESPONDENCE.

I. Together with the Spectator's telescopic and daring views of the Land question, given in last Fors, I may as well preserve its immediate and microscopic approval of our poor little practice upon it at Hincksey :—

"ADAM AND JEHU —It is very vexatious, but one never gets fairly the better of Mr. Ruskin. Sometimes he lets his intellect work, and fires off pamphlet after pamphlet on political economy, each new one more ridiculous than the last, till it ceases to be possible even to read his brochures without condemning them as the utterances of a man who cannot lose a certain eloquence of expression. BUT WHO CANNOT THINK AT ALL; and then, again, he lets his genius work, and produces something which raises the admiration of the reader till every folly which preceded it is forgotten There never was a more absurd paper published than his on the duty of the State towards unmarried couples, and never perhaps one wiser than his lecture on 'Ambition,' reviewed in our columns on the 18th of October, 1873. Just recently he has been pushing some plans for an agricultural Utopia, free of steam-engines and noises and everything modern, in which the inconsequence of his mind is as evident as its radical benevolence; and now he has, we believe, done the whole youth of Oxford a substantial service. He has turned, or rather tried to turn, the rage for athletics into a worthy channel."—*Spectator*, *May* 30, 1874.

The above paragraph may, I think, also be, some day, interesting as a summary of the opinions of the British press on *Fors Clavigera*, and if my last month's letter should have the fortune to displease, or discomfort, any British landlord, my alarmed or offended reader may be relieved and pacified by receiving the Spectatorial warrant at once for the inconsequence of my mind, and for its radical benevolence.

II. The following paragraphs from a leading journal in our greatest commercial city, surpass, in folly and impudence, anything I have yet seen of the kind, and are well worth preserving :—

" The material prosperity of the country has, notwithstanding, increased, and the revenue returns, comparing as they do against an exceptionally high rate of production and consumption, show that we are fairly holding our own." Production and consumption of *what*, Mr. Editor, is the question, as I have told you many a time. A high revenue, raised on the large production and consumption of weak cloth and strong liquor, does *not* show the material prosperity of the country. Suppose you were to tax the production of good pictures, good books, good houses, or honest men, where would your revenue be? " Amongst the middle classes, exceptionally large fortunes have been rapidly realized here and there, chiefly in the misty regions of 'finance,' [What do you mean by misty, Mr. Editor? It is a Turnerian and Titianesque quality, not in the least properly applicable to any cotton-mill business] and instances occur from day to day of almost prodigal expenditure in objects of art [Photographs of bawds, do you mean, Mr. Editor? I know no other objects of art that are multiplying,—certainly not Titians, by your Spectator's decision] and luxury, the display of wealth in the metropolis being more striking year by year.

" Turning from these dazzling exhibitions, the real source of congratulation must be found in the existence of a broad and solid foundation for our apparent prosperity; and this, happily, is represented in the amelioration of the condition of the lower orders of society."—Indeed!

"The adjustment of an increasing scale of wages has not been reduced to scientific principles, and has consequently been more or less arbitrary and capricious. From time to time it has interfered with the even current of affairs, and been resented as an unfair and unwarranted interception of profits in their way to the manufacturer's pockets.

"Whilst 'financial' talent has reaped liberal results from its exercise, the steady productions of manufacturers have left only moderate returns to their producers, and importers of raw material have, as a rule, had a trying time. The difficulties of steamship owners have been tolerably notorious, and the enhancement of sailing vessels is an instance of the adage that 'It is an ill wind that blows no one any good.'

"For our railways, the effects of a most critical half-year can scarcely be forecast. Increased expenses have not, it is to be feared, been met by increased rates and traffics, and the public may not have fully prepared themselves for diminished dividends. With the Erie and the Great Western of Canada undergoing the ordeal of investigation, and the Atlantic and Great Western on the verge of insolvency, it is not surprising that American and colonial railways are at the moment out of favour. If, however, they have not made satisfactory returns to their shareholders, they have been the media of great profit to operators on the stock exchanges; and some day we shall, perhaps, learn the connection existing between the well or ill doing of a railway *per se*, and the facility for speculation in its stock."—*Liverpool Commercial News*, of this year. I have not kept the date.

III. A young lady's letter about flowers and books, I gratefully acknowledge, and have partly answered in the text of this Fors;

the rest she will find answered up and down afterwards, as I can ; also a letter from a youth at New Haven in Connecticut has given me much pleasure. I am sorry not to be able to answer it more specially, but have now absolutely no time for any private correspondence, except with personal friends,—and I should like even those to show themselves friendly rather by setting themselves to understand my meaning in Fors, and by helping me in my purposes, than by merely expressing anxiety for my welfare, not satisfiable but by letters, which do not promote it.

IV. Publishing the subjoined letter from Mr. Sillar, I must now wish him good success in his battle, and terminate my extracts from his letters, there being always some grave points in which I find myself at issue with him, but which I have not at present any wish farther to discuss .—

" I am right glad to see you quote in your July Fors, from the papers which the Record newspaper refused to insert, on the plea of their ' confusing two things so essentially different as usury and interest of money.'

" I printed them, and have sold *two*,—following your advice, and not advertising them.

" You wrong me greatly in saying that I think the sin of usury means every other. What I say is that it is the only sin I know *which is never denounced from the pulpit*, and therefore *I* have to do *that part* of the parson's work. I would much rather be following the business to which I was educated ; but so long as usury is prevalent, honourable and profitable employments *in that business are impossible.* It may be conducted honourably, but at an annual loss ; or it may be conducted profitably *at the expense of honour.* I can no longer afford the former, still less can I afford the latter ; and as I cannot be idle, I occupy my leisure, at least part of it, in a war to the knife with that great dragon 'Debt.' I war not with flesh and blood, but with principalities and powers of darkness in high places."

V. To finish, here is one of the pleasantest paragraphs I ever saw in print :—

"Rope Cordage.—On Saturday last a very interesting experiment was made at Kirkaldy's Testing Works, Southwark Street, as to the relative strength of hand-spun yarn rope, machine yarn rope, and Russian yarn rope. Mr. Plimsoll, M.P., Captain Bedford Pim, M.P., and others attended the test, which lasted over three hours. There were nine pieces of rope, each 10 ft. long, being three of each of the above classes. The ultimate stress or breaking strain of the Russian rope was 11,099 lb., or 1,934 lb. strength per fathom; machine rope, 11,527 lb., or 2,155 lb. per fathom; hand-spun rope, 18,279 lb., or 3,026 lb. per fathom. The ropes were all of 5 in. circumference, and every piece broke clear of the fastenings. The prices paid per cwt. were: Russian rope, 47*s.*; machine yarn rope, 47*s.*; hand-spun yarn rope, 44*s.*—all described as best cordage and London manufacture. It will thus be seen that the hand-made was cheaper by 3*s.* per cwt., and broke at a testing strength of 7,180 lb. over Russian, and 6,752 lb. over machine-made."— *Times,* July 20, 1874.

FORS CLAVIGERA.

LETTER THE 47th.

MINOS RETAINED. THE BRITISH JUDGE.

Hotel du Mont Blanc, St. Martin's,
12th October, 1874

WE have now briefly glanced at the nature of the squire's work in relation to the peasant ; namely, making a celestial or worshipful appearance to him ; and the methods of operation, no less than of appearance, which are generally to be defined as celestial, or worshipful.

We have next to examine by what rules the action of the squire towards the peasant is to be either restrained or assisted ; and the function, therefore, of the lawyer, or definer of limits and modes,—which was above generally expressed, in its relation to the peasant, as "telling him, in black letter, that his house is his own." It will be necessary, however, evidently, that his house *should* be his own, before any lawyer can divinely assert the same to him.

Waiving, for the moment, examination of this primal necessity, let us consider a little how that divine function of asserting, in perfectly intelligible and indelible letters, the absolute claim of a man to his own house, or castle, and all that it properly includes, is actually discharged by the powers of British law now in operation.

We will take, if you please, in the outset, a few wise men's opinions on this matter, though we shall thus be obliged somewhat to generalize the inquiry, by admitting into it some notice of criminal as well as civil law.

My readers have probably thought me forgetful of Sir Walter all this time. No; but all writing about him is impossible to me in the impure gloom of modern Italy. I have had to rest awhile here, where human life is still sacred, before I could recover the tone of heart fit to say what I want to say in this Fors.

He was the son, you remember, of a writer to the signet, and practised for some time at the bar himself. Have you ever chanced to ask yourself what was his innermost opinion of the legal profession ?

Or, have you even endeavoured to generalize that expressed with so much greater violence by Dickens? The latter wrote with a definitely reforming purpose, seemingly ; and, I have heard, had real effects on Chancery practice.

But are the Judges of England—at present I suppose the highest types of intellectual and moral power that Christendom possesses—content to have reform forced on them by the teazing of a caricaturist, instead of the pleading of their own consciences ?

Even if so, is there no farther reform indicated as
necessary, in a lower field, by the same teazing person-
age? The Court of Chancery and Mr. Vholes were not
his only legal sketches. Dodson and Fogg, Sampson
Brass; Serjeant Buzfuz, and, most of all, the examiner,
for the Crown, of Mr. Swiveller in the trial of Kit,*—are
these deserving of no repentant attention? You, good
reader, probably have read the trial in Pickwick, and
the trial of Kit, merely to amuse yourself, and perhaps
Dickens himself meant little more than to amuse you.
But did it never strike you as quite other than a matter
of amusement, that in both cases, the force of the law
of England is represented as employed zealously to
prove a crime against a person known by the accusing
counsel to be innocent; and, in both cases, as obtaining
a conviction?

You might perhaps think that these were only examples of the ludicrous, and sometimes tragic, accidents
which must sometimes happen in the working of any
complex system, however excellent They are by no
means so. Ludicrous, and tragic, mischance must indeed
take place in all human affairs of importance, however
honestly conducted. But here you have deliberate,
artistic, energetic dishonesty; skilfullest and resolutest
endeavour to prove a crime against an innocent person,
—a crime of which, in the case of the boy, the re-

---

* See the part of examination respecting communication held with the
brother of the prisoner.

puted commission will cost him at least the prosperity and honour of his life,—more to him than life itself. And this you forgive, or admire, because it is not done in malice, but for money, and in pride of art. Because the assassin is paid, — makes his living in that line of business,—and delivers his thrust with a bravo's artistic finesse, you think him a respectable person ; so much better in style than a passionate one who does his murder gratis, vulgarly, with a club,— Bill Sikes, for instance ? It is all balanced fairly, as the system goes, you think. ' It works round, and two and two make four. He accused an innocent person to-day :—to-morrow he will defend a rascal.'

And you truly hold this a business to which your youth should be bred—gentlemen of England ?

' But how is it to be ordered otherwise ? Every supposed criminal ought surely to have an advocate, to say what can be said in his favour ; and an accuser, to insist on the evidence against him. Both do their best, and can anything be fairer ? '

Yes ; something else could be much fairer ; but we will find out what Sir Walter thinks, if we can, before going farther , though it will not be easy—for you don't at once get at the thoughts of a great man, upon a great matter.

The first difference, however, which, if you know your Scott well, strikes you, between him and Dickens, is that your task of investigation is chiefly pleasant, though serious; not a painful one——and still less a jesting or mocking one The first figure that rises before you is Pleydell; the second, Scott's own father, Saunders Fairford, with his son. And you think for an instant or two, perhaps, "The question is settled, as far as Scott is concerned, at once. What a beautiful thing is Law!"

For you forget, by the sweet emphasis of the divine art on what is good, that there ever was such a person in the world as Mr. Glossin. And you are left, by the grave cunning of the divine art, which reveals to you no secret without your own labour, to discern and unveil for yourself the meaning of the plot of Redgauntlet.

You perhaps ,were dissatisfied enough with the plot, when you read it for amusement. Such a childish fuss about nothing! Solway sands, forsooth, the only scenery; and your young hero of the story frightened to wet his feet; and your old hero doing nothing but ride a black horse, and make himself disagreeable; and all that about the house in Edinburgh so dull, and no love-making, to speak of, anywhere!

Well, it doesn't come in exactly with my subject, to-day,—but, by the way, I beg you to observe that there is a bit of love in Redgauntlet which is worth any quantity of modern French or English amatory novels in a heap. Alan Fairford has been bred, and willingly bred, in the strictest discipline of mind and conduct; he is an entirely strong, entirely prudent, entirely pure young Scotchman,—and a lawyer Scott, when he wrote the book, was an old Scotchman; and had seen a good deal of the world. And he is going to tell you how Love ought first to come to an entirely strong, entirely prudent, entirely pure youth, of his own grave profession.

How love *ought* to come, mind you. Alan Fairford is the real hero (next to Nanty Ewart) of the novel; and he is the exemplary and happy hero—Nanty being the suffering one, under hand of Fate.

Of course, you would say, if you didn't know the book, and were asked what should happen—(and with Miss Edgeworth to manage matters instead of Scott, or Shakespeare, nothing else *would* have happened,)—of course the entirely prudent young lawyer will consider what an important step in life marriage is; and will look out for a young person of good connections, whose qualities of mind and moral disposition he will examine strictly before allowing his affections to be engaged; he will then consider what income is necessary for a person in a high legal position, etc., etc., etc.

Well, this is what *does* happen, according to Scott, you know;—(or more likely, I'm afraid, know nothing about it). The old servant of the family announces, with some dryness of manner, one day, that a 'leddy' wants to see Maister Alan Fairford,—for legal consultation. The prudent young gentleman, upon this, puts his room into the most impressive order, intending to make a first appearance reading a legal volume in an abstracted state of mind. But, on a knock coming at the street door, he can't resist going to look out at the window; and—the servant maliciously showing in the client without announcement—is discovered peeping out of it. The client is closely veiled—little more than the tip of her nose discernible. She is, fortunately, a little embarrassed herself; for she did not want Mr. Alan Fairford at all, but Mr. Alan Fairford's father. They sit looking at each other—at least, he looking at the veil and a green silk cloak—for half a minute. The young lady—(for she *is* young; he has made out that, he admits; and something more perhaps,)—is the first to recover her presence of mind; makes him a pretty little apology for having mistaken him for his father; says that, now she has done it, he will answer her purpose, perhaps, even better; but she thinks it best to communicate the points on which she requires his assistance, in writing,—curtsies him, on his endeavour to remonstrate, gravely and inexorably into silence,—disappears,—"And put the sun in her pocket, I believe," as she turned the corner, says prudent Mr. Alan And keeps it in her pocket for him,—evermore. That is the way one's Love is sent, when she is sent from Heaven, says the aged Scott.

'But how ridiculous,—how entirely unreasonable,—how

unjustifiable, on any grounds of propriety or common sense!'

Certainly, my good sir,—certainly: Shakespeare and Scott can't help that;—all they know is,—that is the way God and Nature manage it. Of course, Rosalind ought to have been much more particular in her inquiries about Orlando;—Juliet about the person masqued as a pilgrim; —and there is really no excuse whatever for Desdemona's conduct; and we all know what came of it;—but, again I say, Shakespeare and Scott can't help that.

Nevertheless, Love is not the subject of this novel of Redgauntlet; but Law: on which matter we will endeavour now to gather its evidence.

Two youths are brought up together—one, the son of a Cavalier, or Ghibelline, of the old school, whose Law is in the sword, and the heart; and the other of a Roundhead, or Guelph, of the modern school, whose Law is in form and precept. Scott's own prejudices lean to the Cavalier; but his domestic affections, personal experience, and sense of equity, lead him to give utmost finish to the adverse character. The son of the Cavalier—in moral courage, in nervous power, in general sense and self-command,—is entirely inferior to the son of the Puritan; nay, in many respects quite weak and effeminate; one slight and scarcely noticeable touch, (about the unproved pistol,) gives the true relation of the characters, and makes their portraiture complete, as by Velasquez

The Cavalier's father is dead, his uncle asserts the Cavalier's law of the Sword over him, its effects upon him are the first clause of the book.

The Puritan's father — living — asserts the law of Precept over him, its effects upon him are the second clause of the book.

Together with these studies of the two laws in their influence on the relation of guardian and ward—or of father and child, their influence on society is examined in the opposition of the soldier and hunter to the friend of man and animals,—Scott putting his whole power into the working out of this third clause of the book.

Having given his verdict in these three clauses, wholly in favour of the law of precept,—he has to mark the effects of its misapplication,—first moral, then civil.

The story of Nanty Ewart, the fourth clause, is the most instructive and pathetic piece of Scott's judgment on the abuse of the moral law, by pride, in Scotland, which you can find in all his works.

Finally, the effects of the abuse of the civil law by sale, or simony, have to be examined; which is done in the story of Peter Peebles.

The involution of this fifth clause with that of Nanty Ewart is one of the subtlest pieces of heraldic quartering which you can find in all the Waverley novels, and no others have any pretence to range with them in this point of art at all. The best, by other masters, are a mere play of kaleidoscope colour compared to the severe heraldic delineation of the Waverleys.

We will first examine the statement of the abuse of Civil Law.

There is not, if you have any true sympathy with humanity, extant for you a more exquisite study of the relations which must exist, even under circumstances of great difficulty and misunderstanding, between a good father and a good son, than the scenes of Redgauntlet laid in Edinburgh. The father's intense devotion, pride, and joy, mingled with fear, in the son ; the son's direct, unflinching, unaffected obedience, hallowed by pure affection, tempered by youthful sense, guided by high personal power. And all this force of noble passion and effort, in both, is directed to a single object—the son's success at the bar. That success, as usually in the legal profession, must if it be not wholly involved, at least give security for itself, in the impression made by the young counsel's opening speech. All the interests of the reader (if he has any interest in him) are concentrated upon this crisis in the story, and the chapter which gives account of the fluctuating event is one of the supreme masterpieces of European literature.

The interests of the reader, I say, are concentrated on the success of the young counsel : that of his client is of no importance whatever to any one. You perhaps forget even who the client is—or recollect him only as a poor drunkard, who must be kept out of the way for fear he should interrupt his own counsel, or make the jury laugh at him. His cause has been—no one knows how long—in the courts ; it is good for practising on, by any young hand.

You forget Peter Peebles, perhaps : you don't forget Miss Flite, in the Dickens' court ? Better done, therefore,—Miss Flite,—think you ?

No ; not so well done ; or anything like so well done. The very primal condition in Scott's type of the ruined creature is, that he *should* be forgotten ! Worse ;—that he should *deserve* to be forgotten. Miss Flite interests you—takes your affections—deserves them. Is mad, indeed, but not a destroyed creature, morally, at all. A very sweet, kind creature,—not even altogether unhappy,—enjoying her lawsuit, and her bag, and her papers. She is a picturesque, quite unnatural and unlikely figure,—therefore wholly ineffective except for story-telling purposes.

But Peter Peebles is a natural ruin, and a total one. An accurate type of what is to be seen every day, and carried to the last stage of its misery. He is degraded alike in body and heart ;—mad, but with every vile sagacity unquenched,—while every hope in earth and heaven is taken away. And in this desolation, you can only hate, not pity him.

That, says Scott, is the beautiful operation of the

Civil Law of Great Britain, on a man whose affairs it has spent its best intelligence on, for an unknown number of years. His affairs being very obscure, and his cause doubtful, you suppose? No. His affairs being so simple that the young *honest* counsel can explain them entirely in an hour;—and his cause absolutely and unquestionably just.

What is Dickens' entire Court of Chancery to that? With all its dusty delay,—with all its diabolical ensnaring;—its pathetic death of Richard—widowhood of Ada, etc, etc.? All mere blue fire of the stage, and dropped footlights; no real tragedy.—A villain cheats a foolish youth, who would be wiser than his elders, who dies repentant, and immediately begins a new life,—so says, at least, (not the least believing,) the pious Mr. Dickens. All that might happen among the knaves of any profession.

But with Scott, the best honour—soul—intellect in Scotland take in hand the cause of a man who comes to them justly, necessarily, for plain, instantly possible, absolutely deserved, decision of a manifest cause.

They are endless years talking of it,—to amuse, and pay, themselves.

And they drive him into the foulest death—eternal—if there be, for such souls, any Eternity. On which Scott does not feel it his duty, as Dickens does, to offer you an opinion. He tells you, as Shakespeare, the fact he knows,—no more.

There, then, you have Sir Walter's opinion of the existing method and function of British Civil Law.

What the difference may be, and what the consequences of such difference between this lucrative function, and the true duty of Civil Law,—namely, to fulfil and continue in all the world the first mission of the mightiest Lawgiver, and declare that on such and such conditions, written in eternal letters by the finger of God, every man's house, or piece of Holy land, is his own,—there does not, it appears, exist at present wit enough under all the weight of curled and powdered horsehair in England, either to reflect, or to define

In the meantime, we have to note another question beyond, and greater than this,—answered by Scott in his story.

So far as human laws have dealt with the man, this their ruined client has been destroyed in his innocence But there is yet a Divine Law, controlling the injustice of men.

And the historian—revealing to us the full relation of private and public act—shows us that the wretch's destruction was in his refusal of the laws of God, while he trusted in the laws of man.

Such is the entire plan of the story of Redgauntlet, —only in part conscious,—partly guided by the Fors which has rule over the heart of the noble king in his word, and of the noble scribe in his scripture, as over the rivers of water. We will trace the detail of this story farther in next Fors; meantime, here is your own immediate lesson, reader, whoever you may be, from our to-day's work.

The first—not the chief, but the first—piece of good work a man has to do is to find rest for himself,—a place for the sole of his foot; his house, or piece of Holy land; and to *make* it so holy and happy, that if by any chance he receive order to leave it, there may be bitter pain in obedience; and also that to his daughter there may yet one sorrowful sentence be spoken in her day of mirth, "Forget also thy people, and thy father's house."

' But I mean to make money, and have a better and better house, every ten years.'

Yes, I know you do.

If you intend to keep that notion, I have no word more to say to you. Fare you—not well, for you cannot; but as you may.

But if you have sense, and feeling, determine what sort of a house will be fit for you; determine to work for it—to get it—and to die in it, if the Lord will.

' What sort of house will be fit for me?—but of course the biggest and finest I can get will be fittest!'

Again, so says the Devil to you: and if you believe him, he will find you fine lodgings enough,—for rent. But if you don't believe him, consider, I repeat, what sort of house will be fit for you.

'Fit!—but what do you mean by fit?'

I mean, one that you can entirely enjoy and manage; but which you will not be proud of, except as you make it charming in its modesty. If you are proud of it, it is *un*fit for you,—better than a man in your station of life can by simple and sustained exertion obtain; and it should be rather under such quiet level than above. Ashesteil was entirely fit for Walter Scott, and Walter Scott was entirely happy there. Abbotsford was fit also for *Sir* Walter Scott; and had he been content with it, his had been a model life. But he would fain still add field to field,—and died homeless. Perhaps Gadshill was fit for Dickens; I do not know enough of him to judge; and he knew scarcely anything of himself. But the story of the boy on Rochester Hill is lovely.

And assuredly, my aunt's house at Croydon was fit for her; and my father's at Herne Hill,—in which I correct the press of this Fors, sitting in what was once my nursery,—was exactly fit for him, and me. He left it for the larger one—Denmark Hill; and never had a quite happy day afterwards. It was not his fault, the house at Herne Hill was built on clay, and the doctors said he was not well there; also, I was his pride, and he wanted to leave *me* in a better house,—a good father's cruellest, subtlest temptation.

But *you* are a poor man, you say, and have no hope of a grand home?

Well, here is the simplest ideal of operation, then. You dig a hole, like Robinson Crusoe; you gather sticks for fire, and bake the earth you get out of your hole,—partly into bricks, partly into tiles, partly into pots. If there are any stones in the neighbourhood, you drag them together, and build a defensive dyke round your hole or cave. If there are no stones, but only timber, you drive in a palisade. And you are already exercising the arts of the Greeks, Etruscans, Normans, and Lombards, in their purest form, on the wholesome and true threshold of all their art; and on your own wholesome threshold.

You don't know, you answer, how to make a brick, a tile, or a pot; or how to build a dyke, or drive a stake that will stand. No more do I. Our education has to begin;—mine as much as yours. I have indeed, the newspapers say, a power of expression; but as they also say I cannot think at all, you see I have nothing to express; so that peculiar power, according to *them*, is of no use to me whatever.

But you don't want to make your bricks yourself; you want to have them made for you by the United Grand Junction Limited Liability Brick-without-Straw Company, paying twenty-five per cent. to its idle shareholders? Well, what will you do, yourself, then? Nothing? Or do you mean to play on the fiddle to the Company making your bricks? What will *you* do— of this first work necessary for your life? There's nothing but digging and cooking now remains to be done. Will you dig, or cook? Dig, by all means; but your house should be ready for you first.

Your wife should cook. What else can *you* do? Preach?—and give us your precious opinions of God and His ways! Yes, and in the meanwhile *I* am to build your house, am I? and find you a barrel-organ, or a harmonium, to twangle psalm-tunes on, I suppose? Fight—will you?—and pull other people's houses down; while I am to be set to build your barracks, that you may go smoking and spitting about all day, with a cockscomb on your head, and spurs to your heels?— (I observe, by the way, the Italian soldiers have now got cocks' *tails* on their heads, instead of cocks' combs.) —Lay down the law to me in a wig,—will you? and tell me the house I have built is—NOT mine? and take my dinner from me, as a fee for *that* opinion? Build, my man,—build, or dig,—one of the two; and then eat your honestly-earned meat, thankfully, and let other people alone, if you can't help them.

NOTES AND CORRESPONDENCE.

———◆———

The points suggested by the letter printed in the Fors of September, respecting the minor action of English Magistracy, must still be kept for subsequent consideration, our to day's work having been too general to reach them

I have an interesting letter from a man of business, remonstrating with me on my declaration that railroads should no more pay dividends than carriage roads, or field footpaths.

He is a gentle man of business, and meshed, as moderately well-meaning people, nowadays, always are, in a web of equivocation between what is profitable and benevolent.

He says that people who make railroads should be rewarded by dividends for having acted so benevolently towards the public, and provided it with these beautiful and easy means of locomotion But my correspondent is too good a man of business to remain in this entanglement of brains—unless by his own fault. He knows perfectly well, in his heart, that the ' benevolence ' involved in the construction of railways amounts exactly to this much and no more,—that if the British public were informed that engineers were now confident, after their practice in the Cenis and St. Gothard tunnels, that they could make a railway to Hell,—the British public would instantly invest in the concern to any amount, and stop church-building all over the country, for fear of diminishing the dividends.

FORS CLAVIGERA.

LETTER THE 48th.
THE ADVENT COLLECT.

THE accounts of the state of St. George's Fund, given without any inconvenience in crowding type, on the last leaf of this number of Fors, will, I hope, be as satisfactory to my subscribers as they are to me. In these days of financial operation, the subscribers to *anything* may surely be content when they find that all their talents have been laid up in the softest of napkins ; and even farther, that, though they are getting no interest themselves, that lichenous growth of vegetable gold, or mould, is duly developing itself on their capital.

The amount of subscriptions received, during the four years of my mendicancy, might have disappointed me, if, in my own mind, I had made any appointments on the subject, or had benevolence pungent enough to make me fret at the delay in the commencement of the national felicity which I propose to bestow. On the contrary, I am only too happy to continue amusing myself in my study, with stones and pictures ; and find,

as I grow old, that I remain resigned to the conscious-
ness of any quantity of surrounding vice, distress and
disease, provided only the sun shine in at my window
over Corpus Garden, and there are no whistles from
the luggage trains passing the Waterworks.

I understand this state of even temper to be what
most people call ' rational ;' and, indeed, it has been the
result of very steady effort on my own part to keep
myself, if it might be, out of Hanwell, or that other
Hospital which makes the name of Christ's native village
dreadful in the ear of London. For, having long observed that the most perilous beginning of trustworthy
qualification for either of those establishments consisted
in an exaggerated sense of self-importance , and being
daily compelled, of late, to value my own person and
opinions at a higher and higher rate, in proportion to
my extending experience of the rarity of any similar
creatures or ideas among mankind, it seemed to me
expedient to correct this increasing conviction of my
superior wisdom, by companionship with pictures I could
not copy, and stones I could not understand :—while, that
this wholesome seclusion may remain only self-imposed,
I think it not a little fortunate for me that the few
relations I have left are generally rather fond of me ,—
don't know clearly which is the next of kin,—and
perceive that the administration of my inconsiderable
effects* would be rather troublesome than profitable to

* See statement at close of accounts.

them Not in the least, therefore, wondering at the
shyness of my readers to trust me with money of theirs,
I have made, during these four years past, some few
experiments with money of my own,—in hopes of being
able to give such account of them as might justify a
more extended confidence. I am bound to state that the
results, for the present, are not altogether encouraging.
On my own little piece of mountain ground at Coniston
I grow a large quantity of wood-hyacinths and heather,
without any expense worth mentioning ; but my only
industrious agricultural operations have been the getting
three pounds ten worth of hay, off a field for which I
pay six pounds rent ; and the surrounding, with a costly
wall six feet high, to keep out rabbits, a kitchen garden,
which, being terraced and trim, my neighbours say is
pretty ; and which will probably, every third year, when
the weather is not wet, supply me with a dish of strawberries

At Carshalton, in Surrey, I have indeed had the
satisfaction of cleaning out one of the springs of the
Wandel, and making it pleasantly habitable by trout ,
but find that the fountain, instead of taking care of
itself when once pure, as I expected it to do, requires
continual looking after, like a child getting into a mess ;
and involves me besides in continual debate with the
surveyors of the parish, who insist on letting all the
roadwashings run into it. For the present, however, I
persevere, at Carshalton, against the wilfulness of the

spring and the carelessness of the parish ; and hope to conquer both . but I have been obliged entirely to abandon a notion I had of exhibiting ideally clean street pavement in the centre of London,—in the pleasant environs of Church Lane, St. Giles's. There I had every help and encouragement from the authorities ; and hoped, with the staff of two men and a young rogue of a crossing-sweeper, added to the regular force of the parish, to keep a quarter of a mile square of the narrow streets without leaving so much as a bit of orange-peel on the footway, or an eggshell in the gutters. I failed, partly because I chose too difficult a district to begin with, (the contributions of transitional mud being constant, and the inhabitants passive,) but chiefly because I could no more be on the spot myself, to give spirit to the men, when I left Denmark Hill for Coniston.

I next set up a tea-shop at 29, Paddington Street, W., (an establishment which my Fors readers may as well know of,) to supply the poor in that neighbourhood with pure tea, in packets as small as they chose to buy, without making a profit on the subdivision,—larger orders being of course equally acceptable from anybody who cares to promote honest dealing. The result of this experiment has been my ascertaining that the poor only like to buy their tea where it is brilliantly lighted and eloquently ticketed , and as I resolutely refuse to compete with my neighbouring tradesmen either in gas or rhetoric, the patient subdivision of my parcels by the two old servants of my mother's, who manage the business for me, hitherto passes little recognized as an advantage by my uncalculating public. Also, steady increase in the consumption of spirits throughout the neighbourhood faster and faster slackens the demand for tea; but I believe none of these circumstances have checked my trade so much as my own procrastination in painting my sign. Owing to that total want of imagination and invention which makes me so impartial and so accurate a writer on subjects of political economy, I could not for months determine whether the said sign should be of a Chinese character, black upon gold, or of a Japanese, blue upon white; or of pleasant English, rose colour on green; and still less how far legible scale of letters could be compatible, on a board only a foot broad, with lengthy enough elucidation of the peculiar offices of 'Mr. Ruskin's tea-shop.' Meanwhile the business languishes, and the rent and taxes absorb the profits, and something more, after the salary of my good servants has been paid.

In all these cases, however, I can see that I am defeated only because I have too many things on hand: and that neither rabbits at Coniston, road-surveyors at Croydon, or mud in St. Giles's would get the better of me, if I could give exclusive attention to any one business. meantime, I learn the difficulties which are to be met, and shall make the fewer mistakes when I venture on any work with other people's money.

I may as well, together with these confessions, print a piece written for the end of a Fors letter at Assisi, a month or two back, but for which I had then no room, referring to the increase of commercial, religious, and egotistic insanity,* in modern society, and delicacy of the distinction implied by that long wall at Hanwell, between the persons inside it, and out.

'Does it never occur to me,' (thus the letter went on) 'that I may be mad myself?'

Well, I am so alone now in my thoughts and ways, that if I am not mad, I should soon become so, from mere solitude, but for my *work*. But it must be manual work. Whenever I succeed in a drawing, I am happy, in spite of all that surrounds me of sorrow. It is a strange feeling ;—not gratified vanity : I can have any quantity of praise I like from some sorts of people ; but that does me no vital good, (though dispraise does me mortal harm) ; whereas to succeed to my own satisfaction in a manual piece of work, is life,—to me, as to all men ; and it is only the peace which comes necessarily from manual labour which in all time has kept the honest country people patient in their task of maintaining the rascals who live in towns. But we are in hard times, now, for all men's wits ; for men who know the truth are like to go mad from isolation ; and the fools are all going mad in ' Schwarmerei,'—only that is much the pleasanter way. Mr. Lecky, for instance, quoted in

* See second letter in Notes and Correspondence.

last Fors; how pleasant for him to think he is ever so much wiser than Aristotle; and that, as a body the men of his generation are the wisest that ever were born—giants of intellect, according to Lord Macaulay, compared to the pigmies of Bacon's time, and the minor pigmies of Christ's time, and the minutest of all, the miscroscopic pigmies of Solomon's time, and, finally, the vermicular and infusorial pigmies—twenty-three millions to the cube inch—of Mr. Darwin's time, whatever that may be. How pleasant for Mr. Lecky to live in these days of the Anakim,—"his spear, to equal which, the tallest pine," etc., etc., which no man Stratford-born could have lifted, much less shaken.

But for us of the old race—few of us now left,— children who reverence our fathers, and are ashamed of ourselves, comfortless enough in that shame, and yearning for one word or glance from the graves of old, yet knowing ourselves to be of the same blood, and recognizing in our hearts the same passions, with the ancient masters of humanity,—we, who feel as men, and not as carnivorous worms; we, who are every day recognizing some inaccessible height of thought and power, and are miserable in our shortcomings,—the few of us now standing here and there, alone, in the midst of this yelping, carnivorous crowd, mad for money and lust, tearing each other to pieces, and starving each other to death, and leaving heaps of their dung and ponds of their spittle on every palace floor and altar stone,—

it is impossible for us, except in the labour of our hands, not to go mad.

And the danger is tenfold greater for a man in my own position, concerned with the arts which develope the more subtle brain sensations; and, through them, tormented all day long. Mr. Leslie Stephen rightly says how much better it is to have a thick skin and a good digestion. Yes, assuredly; but what is the use of knowing that, if one hasn't? In one of my saddest moods, only a week or two ago, because I had failed twice over in drawing the lifted hand of Giotto's ' Poverty;' utterly beaten and comfortless, at Assisi, I got some wholesome peace and refreshment by mere sympathy with a Bewickian little pig in the roundest and conceitedest burst of pig-blossom. His servant,—a grave old woman, with much sorrow and toil in the wrinkles of *her* skin, while his was only dimpled in its divine thickness,—was leading him, with magnanimous length of rope, down a grassy path behind the convent; stopping, of course, where he chose. Stray stalks and leaves of eatable things, in various stages of ambrosial rottenness, lay here and there, the convent walls made more savoury by their fumigation, as Mr. Leslie Stephen says the Alpine pines are by his cigar. And the little joyful darling of Demeter shook his curly tail, and munched; and grunted the goodnaturedest of grunts, and snuffled the approvingest of snuffles, and was a balm and beatification to behold; and I would fain have changed

places with him for a little while, or with Mr. Leslie
Stephen for a little while,—at luncheon, suppose,—anywhere but among the Alps. But it can't be.

HOTEL MEURICE, PARIS,

20th October, 1874.

I interrupt myself, for an instant or two, to take notice
of two little things that happen to me here—arriving
to breakfast by night train from Geneva.

Expecting to be cold, I had ordered fire, and sat down
by it to read my letters as soon as I arrived, not noticing
that the little parlour was getting much too hot. Presently,
in comes the chambermaid, to put the bedroom in order,
which one enters through the parlour. Perceiving that I
am mismanaging myself, in the way of fresh air, as she
passes through, " Il fait bien chaud, monsieur, ici," says
she reprovingly, and with entire self-possession. Now that
is French servant-character of the right old school. She
knows her own position perfectly, and means to stay in
it, and wear her little white radiant frill of a cap all
her days. She knows my position also ; and has not
the least fear of my thinking her impertinent because she
tells me what it is right that I should know. Presently
afterwards, an evidently German-importation of waiter
brings me up my breakfast, which has been longer in
appearing than it would have been in old times It
looks all right at first,—the napkin, china, and solid silver
sugar basin, all of the old régime. Bread, butter,—yes, of

the best still Coffee, milk,—all right too. But, at last here is a bit of the new régime. There are no sugar-tongs , and the sugar is of beetroot, and in methodically similar cakes, which I must break with my finger and thumb if I want a small piece, and put back what I don't want for my neighbour, to-morrow.

'Civilization,' this, you observe, according to Professor Liebig and Mr. John Stuart Mill. Not according to old French manners, however.

Now, my readers are continually complaining that I don't go on telling them my plan of life, under the rule of St. George's Company.

I *have* told it them, again and again, in broad terms : agricultural life, with as much refinement as I can enforce in it. But it is impossible to describe what I mean by ' refinement,' except in details which can only be suggested by practical need , and which cannot at all be set down at once.

Here, however, to-day, is one instance. At the best hotel in what has been supposed the most luxurious city of modern Europe,—because people are now always in a hurry to catch the train, they haven't time to use the sugar-tongs, or look for a little piece among differently sized lumps, and therefore they use their fingers ; have bad sugar instead of good, and waste the ground that would grow blessed cherry trees, currant bushes, or wheat, in growing a miserable root as a substitute for the sugar-cane, which God has appointed to grow where cherries, and wheat won't, and to give juice which will freeze into sweet snow as pure as hoar-frost.

Now, on the poorest farm of the St. George's Company, the servants shall have white and brown sugar of the best—or none. If we are too poor to buy sugar, we will drink our tea without , and have suet-dumpling instead of pudding. But among the earliest school lessons, and home lessons, decent behaviour at table will be primarily essential ; and of such decency, one little exact point will be—the neat, patient, and scrupulous use of sugar-tongs instead of fingers. If we are too poor to have silver basins, we will have delf ones ; if not silver tongs, we will have wooden ones ; and the boys of the house shall be challenged to cut, and fit together, the prettiest and handiest machines of the sort they can contrive. In six months you would find more real art fancy brought out in the wooden handles and claws, than there is now in all the plate in London

Now, there's the cuckoo-clock striking seven, just as I sit down to correct the press of this sheet, in my nursery at Herne Hill ; and though I don't remember, as the murderer does in Mr. Crummles' play, having heard a cuckoo-clock strike seven—in my infancy, I do remember, in my favourite ' Frank,' much talk of the housekeeper's cuckoo-clock, and of the boy's ingenuity in mending it. Yet to this hour of seven in the morning, ninth December of my fifty-fifth year,

I haven't the least notion how any such clock says 'Cuckoo,' nor a clear one even of the making of the commonest barking toy of a child's Noah's ark. I don't know how a barrel organ produces music by being ground; nor what real function the pea has in a whistle. Physical science—all this—of a kind which would have been boundlessly interesting to me, as to all boys of mellifluous disposition, if only I had been taught it with due immediate practice, and enforcement of true manufacture, or, in pleasant Saxon, 'handiwork.' But there shall not be on St. George's estate a single thing in the house which the boys don't know how to make, nor a single dish on the table which the girls will not know how to cook.

By the way, I have been greatly surprised by receiving some letters of puzzled inquiry as to the meaning of my recipe, given last year, for Yorkshire Pie. Do not my readers yet at all understand that the whole gist of this book is to make people build their own houses, provide and cook their own dinners, and enjoy both? Something else besides, perhaps; but at least, and at first, those. St. Michael's mass, and Christ's mass, may eventually be associated in your minds with other things than goose and pudding; but Fors demands at first no more chivalry nor Christianity from you than that you build your houses bravely, and earn your dinners honestly, and enjoy them both, and be content with them both. The contentment is the main matter; you may enjoy to any extent, but if you are discontented, your life will be poisoned. The little pig was so comforting to me because he was wholly content to be a little pig ; and Mr. Leslie Stephen is in a certain degree exemplary and comforting to me, because he is wholly content to be Mr. Leslie Stephen ; while I am miserable because I am always wanting to be something else than I am. I want to be Turner ; I want to be Gainsborough ; I want to be Samuel Prout ; I want to be Doge of Venice ; I want to be Pope ; I want to be Lord of the Sun and Moon. The other day, when I read that story in the papers about the dog-fight,* I wanted to be able to fight a bulldog.

Truly, that was the only effect of the story upon me, though I heard everybody else screaming out how horrible it was. What's horrible in it? Of course it is in bad taste, and the sign of a declining era of national honour—as all brutal gladiatorial exhibitions are ; and the stakes and rings of the tethered combat meant precisely, for England, what the stakes and rings of the Theatre of Taormina,—where I saw the holes left for them among the turf, blue with Sicilian lilies, in this last April,— meant, for Greece, and Rome. There might be something loathsome, or something ominous, in such a story, to the old Greeks of the school of Heracles ; who used

---

* I don't know how far it turned out to be true, a fight between a dwarf and a bulldog (both chained to stakes as in Roman days), described at length in some journals

to fight with the Nemean lion, or with Cerberus, when it was needful only, and not for money ; and whom their Argus remembered through all Trojan exile. There might be something loathsome in it, or ominous, to an Englishman of the school of Shakespeare or Scott ; who would fight with men only, and loved his hound. But for you—you carnivorous cheats—what, in dog's or devil's name, is there horrible in it for *you ?* Do you suppose it isn't more manly and virtuous to fight a bulldog, than to poison a child, or cheat a fellow who trusts you, or leave a girl to go wild in the streets ? And don't you live, and profess to live—and even insolently proclaim that there's no other way of living than—by poisoning and cheating ? And isn't every woman of fashion's dress, in Europe, now set the pattern of to her by its prostitutes ?

What's horrible in it ? I ask you, the third time. I hate, myself, seeing a bull-dog ill-treated : for they are the gentlest and faithfullest of living creatures if you use them well. And the best dog I ever had was a bull-terrier, whose whole object in life was to please me, and nothing else ; though, if he found he *could* please me by holding on with his teeth to an inch-thick stick, and being swung round in the air as fast as I could turn, that was his own idea of entirely felicitous existence. I don't like, therefore, hearing of a bulldog's being ill-treated ; but I can tell you a little thing that chanced to me at Coniston the other day, more horrible, in the deep elements of it, than all the dog, bulldog, or bull fights, or baitings, of England, Spain, and California A fine boy, the son of an amiable English clergyman, had come on the coach-box round the Water-head to see me, and was telling me of the delightful drive he had had. "Oh," he said, in the triumph of his enthusiasm, "and just at the corner of the wood, there was *such* a big squirrel! and the coachman threw a stone at it, and nearly hit it!"

'Thoughtlessness—only thoughtlessness'—say you—proud father? Well, perhaps not much worse than that. But how *could* it be much worse? Thoughtless is precisely the chief public calamity of our day; and when it comes to the pitch, in a clergyman's child, of not thinking that a stone hurts what it hits of living things, and not caring for the daintiest, dextrousest, innocentest living thing in the northern forests of God's earth, except as a brown excrescence to be knocked off their branches,—nay, good pastor of Christ's lambs, believe me, your boy had better have been employed in thoughtfully and resolutely stoning St. Stephen—if any St Stephen is to be found in these days, when men not only can't see heaven opened, but don't so much as care to see it shut.

For they, at least, meant neither to give pain nor death without cause,—that unanimous company who stopped their ears,—they, and the consenting bystander who afterwards was sorry for his mistake.

But, on the whole, the time has now come when we must cease throwing of stones either at saints or squirrels, and, as I say, build our own houses with them, honestly set: and similarly content ourselves in peaceable use of iron and lead, and other such things which we have been in the habit of throwing at each other dangerously, in thoughtlessness; and defending ourselves against as thoughtlessly, though in what we suppose to be an ingenious manner. Ingenious or not, will the fabric of our new ship of the Line, 'Devastation,' think you, follow its fabricator in heavenly places, when he dies in the Lord? In such representations as I have chanced to see of probable Paradise, Noah is never without his ark;—holding that up for judgment as the main work of his life. Shall we hope at the Advent to see the builder of the 'Devastation' invite St. Michael's judgment on his better style of naval architecture, and four-foot-six-thick 'armour of light'?

It is to-day the second Sunday in Advent, and all over England, about the time that I write these words, full congregations will be for the second time saying Amen to the opening collect of the Christian year.

I wonder how many individuals of the enlightened public understand a single word of its first clause:

"Almighty God, give us grace that we may cast away the works of darkness, and put upon us the armour of light, now in the time of this mortal life."

How many of them, may it be supposed, have any clear knowledge of what grace is, or of what the works of darkness are which they hope to have grace to cast away; or will feel themselves, in the coming year, armed with any more luminous mail than their customary coats and gowns, hosen and hats? Or again, when they are told to "have no fellowship with the unfruitful works of darkness, but rather reprove them,"—what fellowship do they recognize themselves to have guiltily formed; and whom, or what, will they feel now called upon to reprove?

In last Fors, I showed *you* how the works of darkness were unfruitful;—the precise reverse of the fruitful, or creative, works of Light;—but why in this collect, which you pray over and over again all Advent, do you ask for 'armour' instead of industry? You take your coat off to work in your own gardens; why must you put a coat of mail on, when you are to work in the Garden of God?

Well; because the earthworms in it are big—and have teeth and claws, and venomous tongues. So that the first question for you is indeed, not whether you have a mind to work in it—many a coward has that—but whether you have courage to stand in it, and armour proved enough to stand in.

Suppose you let the consenting bystander who took care of the coats taken off to do that piece of work on St. Stephen, explain to you the pieces out of St. Michael's armoury needful to the husbandman, or Georgos, of God's garden.

"Stand therefore; having your loins girt about with Truth."

That means, that the strength of your backbone depends on your meaning to do true battle.

"And having on the breastplate of Justice."

That means, there are to be no partialities in your heart, of anger or pity ,—but you must only in justice kill, and only in justice keep alive.

"And your feet shod with the preparation of the gospel of Peace."

That means, that where your foot pauses, moves, or enters, there shall be peace; and where you can only shake the dust of it on the threshold, mourning

"Above all, take the shield of Faith."

Of fidelity or obedience to your captain, showing his bearings, argent, a cross gules; your safety, and all the army's, being first in the obedience of faith : and all casting of spears vain against such guarded phalanx.

"And take the helmet of Salvation."

Elsewhere, the *hope* of salvation, that being the defence of your intellect against base and sad thoughts, as the shield of fidelity is the defence of your heart against burning and consuming passions.

"And the sword of the Spirit, which is the Word of God."

That being your weapon of war,—your power of action,

whether with sword or ploughshare , according to the saying of St. John of the young soldiers of Christ, " I have written unto you, young men, because ye are strong, and the Word of God abideth in you." The Word by which the heavens were of old ; and which, being once only Breath, became in man Flesh, 'quickening it by the spirit' into the life which is, and is to come , and enabling it for all the works nobly done by the quick, and following the dead.

And now, finish your Advent collect, and eat your Christmas fare, and drink your Christmas wine, thankfully ; and with understanding that if the supper is holy which shows your Lord's death till He come, the dinner is also holy which shows His life , and if you would think it wrong at any time to go to your own baby's cradle side, drunk, do not show your gladness by Christ's cradle in that manner ; but eat your meat, and carol your carol in pure gladness and singleness of heart , and so gird up your loins with truth, that, in the year to come, you may do such work as Christ can praise, whether He call you to judgment from the quick or dead ; so that among your Christmas carols there may never any more be wanting the joyfullest,—

O sing unto the Lord a new song :

Sing unto the Lord, all the earth.

Say among the heathen that the Lord is King :

The world also shall be stablished that it shall not
  be moved.

Let the heavens rejoice,
And let the earth be glad ;
Let the sea shout, and the fulness thereof
Let the field be joyful, and all that is therein :
Then shall all the trees of the wood rejoice
Before the Lord :
For He cometh, for He cometh to JUDGE THE EARTH :
HE SHALL JUDGE THE WORLD WITH RIGHTEOUSNESS,
AND THE PEOPLE WITH HIS TRUTH.

NOTES AND CORRESPONDENCE.

I. I have kept the following kind and helpful letter for the close of the year :—

"*January* 8, 1874

"Sir,—I have been much moved by a passage in No 37 of Fors Clavigera, in which you express yourself in somewhat desponding terms as to your loneliness in 'life and thought,' now you have grown old You complain that many of your early friends have forgotten or disregarded you, and that you are almost left alone. I cannot certainly be called an early friend, or, in the common meaning of the word, a friend of any time.   But I cannot refrain from telling you that there are 'more than 7,000' in this very 'Christ-defying' England whom you have made your friends by your wise sympathy and faithful teaching.   I, for my own part, owe you a debt of thankfulness not only for the pleasant hours I have spent with you in your books, but also for the clearer views of many of the ills which at present press upon us, and for the methods of cure upon which you so urgently and earnestly insist. I would especially mention · Unto this Last ' as having afforded me the highest satisfaction.   It has ever since I first read it been my text-book of political economy.   I think it is one of the need-fullest lessons for a selfish, recklessly competitive, cheapest-buying and dearest-selling age, that it should be told there are principles deeper, higher, and even more prudent than those by which it is just now governed. It is particularly refreshing to find Christ's truths applied to modern commercial immorality in the trenchant and convincing style which characterizes your much maligned but most valuable book. It has been, let me assure you, appreciated in very unexpected quarters; and one humble person to whom I lent my copy, *being too poor to buy one for himself, actually wrote it out word for word, that he might always have it by him.*"

("What a shame!" thinks the enlightened Mudie-subscriber. "See what comes of his refusing to sell his books cheap."

Yes,—see what comes of it. The dreadful calamity, to another person, of doing once, what I did myself twice—and, in great part of the book, three times. A vain author, indeed, thinks nothing of the trouble of writing his own books. But I had infinitely rather write somebody else's. My good poor disciple, at the most, had not half the pain his master had; learnt his book rightly, and gave me more help, by this best kind of laborious sympathy, than twenty score of flattering friends who tell me what a fine word-painter I am, and don't take the pains to understand so much as half a sentence in a volume.)

"You have done, and are doing, a good work for England, and I pray you not to be discouraged. Continue as you have been doing, convincing us by your 'sweet reasonableness' of our errors and miseries, and the time will doubtless come when your work, now being done in Jeremiah-like sadness and hopelessness, will bear gracious and abundant fruit.

"Will you pardon my troubling you with this note? but, indeed, I could not be happy after reading your gloomy experience, until I had done my little best to send one poor ray of comfort into your seemingly almost weary heart.

"I remain,

"Yours very sincerely."

II Next to this delightful testimony to my 'sweet reasonableness,' here is some discussion of evidence on the other side.—

"November 12, 1872

"To JOHN RUSKIN, LL.D., greeting, these.

"Enclosed is a slip cut from the 'Liverpool Mercury' of last Friday, November 8 I don't send it to you because I think it matters anything what the 'Mercury' thinks about any one's qualification for either the inside or outside of any asylum, but that I may suggest to you, as a working-man reader of your letters, the desirability of your printing any letters of importance you may send to any of the London papers, over again —in, say, the space of 'Fors Clavigera' that you have set apart for correspondence It is most tantalizing to see a bit printed like the enclosed, and not know either what is before or after I felt similar feelings some time ago over a little bit of a letter about the subscription to Warwick Castle

"We cannot always see the London papers, especially us provincials, and we would like to see what goes on between you and the newspaper world

"Trusting that you will give this suggestion some consideration, and at any rate take it as given in good faith from a disciple following afar off,

"I remain, sincerely yours"

The enclosed slip was as follows —

"MR. RUSKIN'S TENDER POINT.—Mr John Ruskin has written a letter to a contemporary on madness and crime, which goes far to clear up the mystery which has surrounded some of his writings of late. The following passage amply qualifies the distinguished art critic for admission into any asylum in the country —'I assure you, sir, insanity is a tender point with me'" The writer then quotes to the end the last paragraph of the letter, which, in compliance with my correspondent's wish, I am happy here to reprint in its entirety.

MADNESS AND CRIME.

TO THE EDITOR OF THE 'PALL MALL GAZETTE.'

Sir,—Towards the close of the excellent article on the Taylor trial in your issue for October 31, you say that people never will be, nor ought to be, persuaded "to treat criminals simply as vermin which they destroy, and not as men who are to be punished." Certainly not, sir! Who ever talked or thought of regarding criminals "simply" as anything; (or innocent people either, if there be any)? But regarding criminals complexly and accurately, they are partly men, partly vermin; what is human in them you must punish—what is vermicular, abolish. Anything between—if you can find it—I wish you joy of, and hope you may be able to preserve it to society. Insane persons, horses, dogs, or cats, become vermin when they become dangerous. I am sorry for darling Fido, but there is no question about what is to be done with him.

Yet, I assure you, sir, insanity is a tender point with me. One of my best friends has just gone mad; and all the rest say I am mad myself. But, if ever I murder anybody—and, indeed, there are numbers of people I should like to murder—I won't say that I ought to be hanged; for I think nobody but a bishop or a bank director can ever be rogue enough to deserve hanging; but I particularly, and with all that is left me of what I imagine to be sound mind, request that I may be immediately shot.

I am, Sir, your obedient servant,

J. RUSKIN.

Corpus Christi College, Oxford, November 2, (1872)

III. I am very grateful to the friend who sends me the follow ing note on my criticism of Dickens in last letter:—

"It does not in the least detract from the force of Fors, p. 253, line 18 (November), that there was a real ' Miss Flite,' whom I have seen, and my father well remembers ; and who used to haunt the Courts in general, and sometimes to address them. She had been ruined, it was believed ; and Dickens must have seen her, for her picture is like the original But he knew nothing about her, and only constructed her after his fashion. She cannot have been any prototype of the character of Miss Flite. I never heard her real name Poor thing ! she did not look sweet or kind, but crazed and spiteful, and unless looks deceived Dickens, he just gave careless, false witness about her Her condition seemed to strengthen your statement in its very gist,—as Law had made her look like Peter Peebles

" My father remembers little Miss F , of whom nothing was known. She always carried papers and a bag, and received occasional charity from lawyers.

" Gridley's real name was Ikey,—he haunted Chancery. Another, named Pitt, in the Exchequer,—broken attorneys, both."

IV. I have long kept by me an official statement of the condition of England when I began Fors, and together with it an illustrative column, printed, without alteration, from the ' Pall Mall Gazette' of the previous year. They may now fitly close my four years' work, of which I have good hope next year to see some fruit

MR. GOSCHEN ON THE CONDITION OF ENGLAND.—" The nation is again making money at an enormous rate, and driving every kind of decently secure investment up to unprecedented figures Foreign Stocks, Indian Stocks, Home Railway Shares, all securities which are beyond the control of mere speculators and offer above four per cent. were never so dear ; risky loans for millions, like that for Peru, are taken with avidity; the cup is getting full, and in all human probability some new burst of speculation is at hand, which may take a beneficial form —for instance, we could get rid of a hundred millions in making cheap country railways with immense advantage—but will more probably turn out to be a mere method of depletion. However it goes, the country is once more getting rich, and the money is filtering downwards to the actual workers. The people, as Mr Goschen showed by unimpugnable figures, are consuming more sugar, more tea, more beer, spirits, and tobacco, more, in fact, of every kind of popular luxury, than ever. Their savings have also increased, while the exports of cotton, of wool, of linen, of iron, of machinery, have reached a figure wholly beyond precedent. By the testimony of all manner of men—factory inspectors, poor-law inspectors, members of great cities—the Lancashire trade, the silk trade, the flax-spinning trade, the lace trade, and, above all, the iron trade, are all so flourishing, that the want is not of work to be done, but of hands to do it. Even the iron shipbuilding trade, which was at so low a point, is reviving, and the only one believed to be still under serious depression is the building trade of London, which has, it is believed, been considerably overdone. So great is the demand for hands in some parts of the country, that Mr. Goschen believes that internal emigration would do more to help the people than emigration to America, while it is certain that no relief which can be afforded by the departure of a few workpeople is equal to the relief caused by the revival of any one great trade—relief, we must add, which would be more rapid and diffused if the trades' unions, in this one respect at least false to their central idea of the brotherhood of labour, were not so jealous of the intrusion of outsiders. There is hardly a trade into which a countryman of thirty, however clever, can enter at his own discretion—one of the many social disqualifications which press upon the agricultural labourer.

"The picture thus drawn by Mr Goschen, and truly drawn— for the President of the Poor-Law Board is a man who does not manipulate figures, but treats them with the reverence of the born statist—is a very pleasant one, especially to those who believe that wealth is the foundation of civilization ; but yet what a weary load it is that, according to the same speech, this country is carrying, and must carry ! There are 1,100,000 paupers on the books, and not a tenth of them will be taken off by any revival whatever, for not a tenth of them are workers. The rest are children—350,000 of them alone— widows, people past work, cripples, lunatics, incapables, human drift of one sort or another, the detritus of commerce and labour, a compost of suffering, help-lessness, and disease. In addition to the burden of the State, in addition to the burden of the Debt, which we talk of as nothing, but without which England would be the least-taxed country in the world, this country has to maintain an army of incapables twice as numerous as the army of France, to feed, and clothe, and lodge and teach them,—an army which she cannot disband, and which she seems incompetent even to diminish. To talk of emigration, of enterprise, even of education, as reducing this burden, is almost waste of breath; for cripples do not emigrate, the aged do not benefit by trade, when education is universal children must still be kept alive."—*The Spectator, June* 25, 1870.

V. The following single column of the 'Pall Mall Gazette' has been occasionally referred to in past letters ·—

" It is proposed to erect a memorial church at Oxford to the late Archbishop Longley. The cost is estimated at from £15,000 to £20,000 The subscriptions promised already amount to upwards of £2,000, and in the list are the Archbishop of Canterbury, and the Bishops of Oxford, St. Asaph, and Chester."

" An inquest was held in the Isle of Dogs by Mr. Humphreys,

the coroner, respecting the death of a woman named Catherine Spence, aged thirty-four, and her infant. She was the wife of a labourer, who had been almost without employment for two years and a half. They had pledged all their clothes to buy food, and some time since part of the furniture had been seized by the brokers for rent. The house in which they lived was occupied by six families, who paid the landlord 5s. 9d. for rent. One of the witnesses stated that 'all the persons in the house were ill off for food, and the deceased never wanted it more than they did.' The jury on going to view the bodies found that the bed on which the woman and child had died was composed of rags, and there were no bed-clothes upon it A small box placed upon a broken chair had served as a table. Upon it lay a tract entitled ' *The Goodness of God.*' The windows were broken, and an old iron tray had been fastened up against one and a board up against another. Two days after his wife's death the poor man went mad, and he was taken to the workhouse. He was not taken to the asylum, for there was no room for him in it—it was crowded with mad people. Another juror said it was of no use to return a verdict of death from starvation. It would only cause the distress in the island to be talked about in newspapers. The jury returned a verdict that the deceased woman died from exhaustion, privation, and want of food."

"The Rev. James Nugent, the Roman Catholic chaplain of the Liverpool borough gaol, reported to the magistrates that crime is increasing among young women in Liverpool; and he despairs of amendment until effective steps are taken to check the open display of vice which may now be witnessed nightly, and even daily, in the thoroughfares of the town. Mr. Raffles, the stipendiary magistrate, confesses that he is at a loss what to do in order to deter women of the class referred to from offending against the law, as even committal to the sessions and a long term of imprisonment fail to produce beneficial effects. Father Nugent also despairs of doing much good with this class; but he thinks that if they were subjected to stricter control, and prevented from parading in our thoroughfares, many girls would be deterred from falling into evil ways."

"At the Liverpool borough gaol sessions Mr. Robertson Gladstone closely interrogated the chaplain (the Rev. Thomas Carter) respecting his visitation of the prisoners. Mr. Gladstone is of opinion that sufficient means to make the prisoners impressionable to religious teaching are not used; whilst the chaplain asserts that the system which he pursues is based upon a long experience, extending over twenty-eight years, at the gaol. Mr. Gladstone, who does not share the chaplain's belief that the prisoners are 'generally unimpressionable,' hinted that some active steps in the matter would probably be taken."

"Mr. Fowler, the stipendiary magistrate of Manchester, referring to Mr. Ernest Jones' death yesterday in the course of the proceedings at the City police-court, said 'I wish to say one word, which I intended to have said yesterday morning, in reference to the taking from amongst us of a face which has been so familiar in this court; but I wished to have some other magistrates present in order that I might, on the part of the bench, and not only as an individual, express our regret at the unexpected removal from our midst of a man whose life has been a very remarkable one, whose name will always be associated in this country in connection with the half-century he lived in it, and who, whatever his faults— and who amongst us is free?—possessed the great virtues of un-doubted integrity and honour, and of being thoroughly consistent, never flinching from that course which he believed to be right, though at times at the cost of fortune and of freedom.'"

"A Chester tradesman named Meacock, an ex-town councillor,

has been arrested in that city on a charge of forging conveyances of property upon which he subsequently obtained a mortgage of £2,200. The lady who owns the property appeared before the magistrates, and declared that her signature to the conveyance was a forgery. The prisoner was remanded, and was sent to prison in default of obtaining the bail which was required."

"Mr. Hughes, a Liverpool merchant, was summoned before the local bench for having sent to the London Dock a case, containing hydrochloric acid, without a distinct label or mark denoting that the goods were dangerous. A penalty of £10 was imposed."

"A woman, named Daley, came before the Leeds magistrates, with her son, a boy six years old, whom she wished to be sent to a reformatory, as she was unable to control him. She said that one evening last week he went home, carrying a piece of rope, and said that he was going to hang himself with it. He added that he had already attempted to hang himself ' in the Crown Court, but a little lass loosed the rope for him, and he fell into a tub of water.' It turned out that the mother was living with a man by whom she had two children, and it was thought by some in court that her object was merely to relieve herself of the cost and care of the boy ; but the magistrates, thinking that the boy would be better away from the contaminating influence of the street and of his home, committed him to the Certifical Industrial Schools until he arrives at sixteen years of age, and ordered his mother to contribute one shilling per week towards his maintenance."—*Pall Mall Gazette, January* 29, 1869.

Subscriptions to St. George's Fund.

TO CLOSE OF YEAR 1874.

(The Subscribers each know his or her number in this List)

		£	s.	d.
1.	Annual, £4 0 0 (1871, '72, '73, '74) .	16	0	0
2.	Annual, £20 0 0 (1871, '72, '73, 74) .	80	0	0
3	Gift	5	0	0
4.	Gifts (1871), £30 0 0; (1873), £20 0 0.	50	0	0
5.	Gift (1872)	20	0	0
6	Annual, £1 1 0 (1872, 73 '74) .	3	3	0
7	Gift (1872) .	10	0	0
8	Annual, £20 0 0 (1872, '73, '74)	60	0	0
9	Gift (1872) .	25	0	0
10	Annual, £5 0 0 (1872, '73)	10	0	0
11	Annual, £1 1 0 (1873, 74)	2	2	0
12	Gift (1873) . . .	4	0	0
13	Annual, £3 0 0 (1873, '74)	6	0	0
14.	Gift (1873) .	13	10	0
15	Gift (1873) .	5	0	0
16	Gift (1874) .	25	0	0
17	,,	1	0	0
18	,,	10	0	0
19	,,	5	0	0
20	,,	2	0	0
21.	,,	10	10	0
22.	,,	1	1	0
23	,,	5	0	0
24	,,	1	1	0
		£370	7	0

One or two more subscriptions have come in since this list was drawn up ; these will be acknowledged in the January number, and the subjoined letter from Mr Cowper-Temple gives the state of the Fund in general terms

BROADLANDS, ROMSEY,
December 9, 1874

DEAR RUSKIN,

The St. George's Fund, of which Sir Thomas Acland and I are Trustees, consists at present of £7,000 * Consolidated Stock, and of £923 standing to the credit of our joint account at the Union Bank of London, Chancery Lane Branch. Contributions to this fund are received by the Bank and placed to the credit of our joint account

Yours faithfully,
W. COWPER-TEMPLE.

---

* I have heard that some impression has got abroad that in giving this £7,000 stock to the St. George's Company, I only parted with one year's income It was a fairly estimated tenth of my entire property including Brantwood The excess of the sum now at the credit of the Trustees, over the amount subscribed, consists in the accumulated interest on this stock With the sum thus at their disposal, the Trustees are about to purchase another £1,000 of stock, and in the 1ors of January will be a more complete statement of what we shall begin the year with, and of some dawning prospect of a beginning also to our operations

BIBLIOLIFE

Old Books Deserve a New Life
www.bibliolife.com

Did you know that you can get most of our titles in our trademark **EasyScript**™ print format? **EasyScript**™ provides readers with a larger than average typeface, for a reading experience that's easier on the eyes.

Did you know that we have an ever-growing collection of books in many languages?

Order online:
www.bibliolife.com/store

Or to exclusively browse our **EasyScript**™ collection:
www.bibliogrande.com

At BiblioLife, we aim to make knowledge more accessible by making thousands of titles available to you – quickly and affordably.

Contact us:
BiblioLife
PO Box 21206
Charleston, SC 29413

1579580R0

Printed in Great Britain by Amazon.co.uk, Ltd., Marston Gate.